D0004504

JEFFERSON

THE ESSENTIAL
Jefferson

Thomas Jefferson

EDITED BY
John Dewey

Dover Publications, Inc., Mineola, New York

Bibliographical Note

This Dover edition, first published in 2008, is an unabridged republication of *The Living Thoughts of Thomas Jefferson,* originally published by Longmans, Green and Co., New York, in 1940. The selections are originally from *The Writings of Thomas Jefferson,* edited by H. A. Washington, New York, in 1853. The woodcut portrait of Jefferson was made by Professor Hans A. Mueller.

Library of Congress Cataloging-in-Publication Data

Jefferson, Thomas, 1743–1826.
    [Living thoughts of Thomas Jefferson]
    The essential Jefferson / Thomas Jefferson ; edited by John Dewey.
        p. cm.
    "Unabridged republication of The living thoughts of Thomas Jefferson, originally published by Longmans, Green and Co., New York, in 1940"—T.p. verso.
    ISBN-13: 978-0-486-46599-9
    ISBN-10: 0-486-46599-3
    1. Jefferson, Thomas, 1743–1826—Quotations. 2. United States—Politics and government—1775–1783—Sources. 3. United States—Politics and government—1783–1809—Sources. I. Dewey, John, 1859–1952. II. Title.

E302.J495 2008
973.4'6092—dc22

                                                                    2007043049

Manufactured in the United States of America
Dover Publications, Inc., 31 East 2nd Street, Mineola, N.Y. 11501

THOMAS JEFFERSON

Thomas Jefferson was fortunate in his birth and early surroundings, being a product both of the aristocracy of the time and of the pioneer frontier. He was fortunate in his contacts and his experiences. The United States is fortunate that he had them. The fact that he occupied certain offices is of little account in itself ; comparative nonentities have been foreign envoys and presidents. The use he made of these positions is what counts, and the use includes not only the political policies he urged and carried through, but even more the observations he made and the reflections they produced. His duties, for example, in Paris were few and not very important, "the receipt of our whale-oils, salted fish and salted meats on favorable terms." But the French Revolution began while he was there and he was its keen and intelligent observer. It is typical of him that the political offices he held are not mentioned in the epitaph he wrote for his tombstone. He wished to be remembered as "the author of the Declaration of Independence, the statute of Virginia for religious liberty, and father of the University of Virginia."

His activities in public life provided for him the opportunity for the experiences which inspired and matured his ideas. His republican convictions were formed early in his life ; they were absorbed into his life upon what was then the western frontier ; they seem to have been crystallized when he was only twenty-two years old by hearing a speech of Patrick Henry in opposition to the British Stamp Act. From that time on he was a leader in every movement for freedom and independence, usually somewhat in advance of other "rebels," finding what he said or wrote disapproved of at the time, only to win later assent. He developed with the experiences enlarged responsibilities gave him, but it was uninterruptedly in one direction. Political expediency may have caused him to deviate on special points, but there are few men in public life whose course has been so straight. Natural sympathies, actual experiences, intellectual principles united to produce a character of singular consistency and charm.

Two days before he retired from the presidency, he wrote to his French friend, de Nemours, as follows : "Nature intended me for the tranquil pursuits of science by rendering them my supreme delight. But the enormities of the times in which I have lived have forced me to take part in resisting them." Later "the hermit of Monticello," as he sometimes called himself, remarked in a passage that comes nearer to tapping a poetical vein than almost anything he ever wrote : "The motion of my blood no longer keeps time with the tumult of the world. It leads me to seek for happiness in the lap and love of my family, in the society of my neighbors and my books, in the wholesome occupation of my farm and my affairs, in an interest or affection in every bud that opens, in every breath that blows around me, in an entire freedom of rest, of motion, of thought, owing account to myself alone of my hours and actions."

I do not quote these passages in order to make them the text for a defense of Jefferson's sincerity, which has been questioned on the ground that while he purported to live in the retirement of a country gentleman, he was in fact the focal point of all policies and movements that maintained the integrity of republican institutions against what seemed to him to invade them in any way. I quote them to illustrate what I believe to be the key to the work and character of our first great democrat : the vital union of attitudes and convictions so spontaneous that they are of the kind called instinctive with fruits of a rich and varied experience : — a union that was cemented by the ceaseless intellectual activity which was his "supreme delight." But in a more conventional way, he was that rare person in politics, an idealist whose native faith was developed, checked, and confirmed by extremely extensive and varied practical experience. It is seldom, I imagine, that an unusually sincere and unified natural temperament has been so happily combined with rich opportunities for observation and reflection. If he left the stamp of his idealism upon the course of events, it is because this experience added realistic substance to the inherent bent of his natural disposition. If it is true, as he wrote to Adams, that "Whig and Tory are terms of natural as well as of civil history," the pages of the latter may be searched to find another man whose native constitution so properly destined him to espouse the liberal cause and whose career so happily furnished the conditions that gave that constitution opportunity for articulate expression in deed and word.

As long as there are different parties in the United States, there will be dispute as to the soundness of the respective political philosophies associated with the names of Hamilton and Jefferson. If Jefferson was right, the source of the difference lies deep in the varying attitudes of human nature. But it would be a great pity if partisan differences are allowed to identify the teachings of these two men with party strife so as to disable us from appreciating the greatness of our common American heritage. We should do well to declare a truce in party controversy till we have congratulated ourselves upon our great good fortune in having two extraordinarily able men formulate the fundamental principles upon which men divide.

Considering the small size of the American population a hundred and fifty, a hundred and twenty years ago, we may well be amazed, as well as grateful, at the spectacle of the intellectual and moral calibre of the men who took a hand in shaping the American political tradition.   The military and moral, although not especially the intellectual, repute of Washington has made him a part of a common heritage.   There are also Jefferson, Hamilton, Madison, followed at some distance by Franklin and John Adams, and at a greater distance by Monroe.   There were giants in those days.   It is more than a pity if either partisan differences or a vague indiscriminate adulation of the Founding Fathers is allowed to produce and create indifference to what they contributed to American institutions and to what we still may learn from them.   There still exists among us a kind of intellectual parochialism which induces us to turn to political philosophers of the old world who do not measure up to the stature of our own political thinkers — to say nothing of their remoteness from our own conditions.

Before speaking specifically of Jefferson's social and moral philosophy, something will be said about the range and depth of Jefferson's interests.   Irrespective of any question of whose political ideas are sound, there is no doubt that Jefferson was the most universal as a human being of all of his American and perhaps European contemporaries also.   We cannot pride ourselves that he was a typical or representative American.   He is too far above the average for that.   But we can say that he embodied in himself typical American characteristics that are usually dispersed.   His curiosity was insatiable.   The passage of Terence, accounting nothing human foreign, made trite by frequent usage, applies with peculiar force to him.   His interest in every new and useful invention was at least equal to that of Franklin ; his sayings are without that tinge of smugness that sometimes colors Franklin's reflections on life.

He occupied practically every possible position of American public life, serving in each not only with distinction but marked power of adaptability to the new and unexpected.

The more one reads his letters and other records, the more surprised is one that a single person could find time and energy for such a range of diverse interests. As a farmer, he kept abreast with every advance in botanical and agricultural theory and practice. His notes of travel in France and Italy include the most detailed observations of soils, crops, domestic animals, farm implements and methods of culture. He is moved by what he sees to design a new mouldboard for a plough, having minimum mechanical resistance. Just before retiring from the presidency he notes with pleasure the invention in France of a plough, which was proved by test with a dynamometer to have increased efficiency. He was busy in correspondence with European societies and individuals in exchange of seeds. Of his introduction of the olive tree into South Carolina and Georgia and of upland rice into the same states, he says, "The greatest service which can be rendered any country is to add a useful plant to its culture ; especially, a bread grain ; next in value to bread is oil."

As far as I have discovered, his inclusion of a professorship of Agriculture in the faculty of the University of Virginia marks the first recognition of the subject for study in higher education. He himself ranked it as of equal importance with the professorship in Government that was provided. The plan he drew up for the institution of a system of Agricultural Societies includes most of the topics now forming the studies of our agricultural colleges, save the problem of marketing. His constant attention to the checking of theory by practical experience is seen in his desire for a report upon "the different practices of husbandry, including the bad as well as the good," with the statement that a selection of all the good ones for imitation and the bad ones for avoidance "would compose a course probably near perfection."

There is no discovery in natural science to the credit of Jefferson similar to that of Franklin in electricity. But his faith in scientific advance as a means of popular enlightenment and of social progress was backed by continual interest in discoveries made by others. When helping his grandson with his scholastic mathematical studies, he writes to a friend that he had resumed that study with great avidity, since it was ever his favorite one, there being no theories, no uncertainties, but all "demonstration and satisfaction." He notes in a letter the superiority of French mathematicians of the time due to their development of analytic methods and expresses his pleasure that English mathematicians are adopting them and are also abandoning the method of fluxions in calculus. His most active interest was in the natural sciences. The foundations of modern chemistry were laid during his life time. Priestley is one of the correspondents with whom Jefferson has closest intellectual sympathy. His "utilitarian" interest is manifested in an expression of regret that chemists had not followed Franklin in directing science to something "useful in private life"; with a hope that their science would be applied to "brewing, making cider, fermentation and distillation generally, making bread, butter, cheese, soap, incubating eggs, etc." He was also skeptical about theories not backed by evidence gained through observation, and thought the French *philosophes*, whose acquaintance he made, indulged in altogether too much unverifiable speculation. He says in one letter: "I am myself an empiric in natural philosophy, suffering my faith to go no further than my facts. I am pleased, however, to see the efforts of hypothetical speculation, because by the

collisions of different hypotheses, truth may be elicited
and science advanced in the end."

Because of the evidence it provides regarding Jefferson's belief in the union of theory and experience —
or practice — it is worth while to quote a passage in
which he expresses his opinion about medicine, the passage being taken from a letter to a physician in which
he explains that he is sending a grandson to Philadelphia to study botany, natural history, anatomy, possibly surgery, but not medicine. "I have myself lived
to see the disciples of Hoffmann, Boerhaave, Stahl,
Cullen, Brown, succeed one another like the shifting
figures of a magic lantern, and their fancies, like the
annual doll-babies from Paris, becoming, from their
novelty, the vogue of the day, and yielding to the next
novelty their ephemeral favor. . . It is in this part of
medicine that I wish to see a reform, an abandonment
of hypothesis for sober facts, the first degree of value
set on clinical observation, and the lowest on visionary
theories. . . The only sure foundations of medicine
are an intimate knowledge of the human body, and observation of the effect of medicinal substances on
that." It is characteristic of him to end his letter with
the following statement : "At any rate the subject has
permitted me for a moment to abstract myself from
the dry and dreary waste of politics, into which I have
been impressed by the times on which I happened, and
to indulge in the rich fields of nature where alone I
should have served as a volunteer, if left to my natural
inclinations and partialities."

It would be a mistake, however, to suppose that Jefferson's interest in science was confined to the field
in which useful applications were favorable. He somehow found time to keep up with progress made in
astronomy ; he made personal observations in the case
of a total eclipse of the sun, obtaining a specially ac-

curate chronometer in order that his observations of times might be accurate ; he recommended the use of platinum in mirrors of telescopes ; he interested himself in the problem of a new method for determining longitude, which he wished to apply also to correction of maps made by ordinary methods of surveying. His letters on weights and measures are quite extensive ; he favored a decimal metric system but was opposed to the French selection of its basis. He expended a good deal of ingenuity in devising a standard pendulum swing as a more natural basis, and seems even to have entertained the hope that his project might — after Bonaparte was defeated in war — take the place of the French system. His geological interest was aroused by the existence of fossils, from bones of mammoths to sea shells found thousands of feet above the sea — a subject on which he rejected all theories advanced at the time, holding that more evidence was required before an adequate theory could be framed. His interest in mineralogy was great but mainly practical, since he thought the controversies between "Vulcanists" and "Neptunians" futile. He regretted the backwardness of meteorology and in addition to keeping weather records himself, urged others to do so.

"Science" is used by Jefferson, in agreement with the habit of his day, as an equivalent of *knowledge*. It included what we now call scholarship as well as what we call science. Jefferson was interested in language theoretically as well as practically. He discussed the contemporary pronunciation of Greek — with which he became acquainted while in Paris — in relation to that of classic Greece. He made a collection of vocabularies of fifty different Indian tribes. He began the collection as part of a project for writing a history of the Indians — in whose fate he took a civilized interest not characteristic of the usual attitude. For thirty years he took every opportunity to obtain from correspondents a list of about two hundred and fifty words, covering such objects and acts as every tribe would have names for. He compared names common to these lists with vocabularies of races in Eastern Europe as they were published in Russia, for he was convinced that "filiation of languages was the best means of studying filiation of peoples." His great and abiding interest in Anglo-Saxon undoubtedly had a political bias. For he was convinced that the liberal element in the British constitution was derived from Anglo-Saxon sources while the Norman sources introduced the "Tory" element. As a reason for introducing Anglo-Saxon into the subjects taught in the University of Virginia, he said "the learners will imbibe with the language their free principles of government."

Finally, it is instructive, if not especially important, to note his attitude on the growth of the English language, his idea on this special point being completely consistent with his general philosophy. After saying he is a foe of purisms and a friend of neologisms, since language grows by their introduction and testing, he says : "Dictionaries are but the depositories of words already legitimated by usage. Society is the workshop in which new ones are elaborated. When an individual uses a new word, if ill formed it is rejected in society ; if well formed, adopted, and after due time laid up in the depository of dictionaries. And if, in this process of sound ne-ologisation, our trans-Atlantic brethren shall not choose to accompany us, we may furnish, after the Ionians, a second example of a colonial dialect improving on its primitive." The principles here expressed are now generally accepted, but I doubt if a half-dozen men in the country were bold enough to assert them when Jefferson gave expression to them.

Jefferson's ideas about the fine arts suffer from his habit of subjecting things in which the old world was more advanced than the new to the test of utility as

a measure of the value of their introduction here.
Only in the case of architecture, gardens, and music
does he allow his own personal taste free manifestation
— and in the former case, motives of utility also enter.
It was, however, a lifelong concern of his, both in
theory and practice.   Of music, he says it is the one
thing in France about which he is tempted to disobey
the Biblical injunction against coveting.   In literature
(in the sense of belles lettres), only the classics command his complete admiration.   He regarded them as
luxuries, but as "sublime" ones.   "Homer in his own
language" was his chief delight and he goes so far as
to say that he thanked God on his knees for directing
his early education so as to put him in "possession of
this rich source of delight."   Of modern poetry, the
following is, as far as I am aware, all he has to say :
"Pope, Dryden, Thomson, Shakspeare, and of the
French, Molière, Racine, the Corneilles, may be read
with pleasure and improvement."   The factor of "improvement" bulked rather large in his mind, since he
seemed to have limited the scope of "luxury" to Greek
and Latin authors. Novels he regarded as mostly a
"mass of trash, fostering bloated imagination, sickly
judgment and disgust toward all the real businesses of
life."   The exceptions he admitted were those which
were "interesting and useful vehicles of a sound morality."   However, while he ranked the writing of Miss
Edgeworth among the latter, he gave the palm to
Sterne.   Nevertheless, external evidence bears out the
truth of his statement (made in a letter to John Adams)
— that he "could not live without books."   While he
was in France, he collected a library by spending
"every afternoon in which I was disengaged in exam-
ining all the principal bookstores, turning over every
book with my own hand, and putting by everything
that related to America and indeed whatever was rare
and valuable in every science."   He attempted to have

the duty on foreign books removed. He introduced bills for establishment of libraries at public expense, and hoped to see a circulating library in every county. It is doubtful if any public man today could quote as freely from the classics as he and John Adams did in their correspondence with each other.

While Jefferson's views on the arts, as on science, reflected the preferences of Franklin — and of Americans generally — for the useful and the practical, his standard of utility and of practical value was that of the benefit of the people as a whole, not that of individuals or of a class. I have quoted in the text a passage from a letter written to John Adams, in which he says that America has given the world "physical liberty"; contribution to "moral emancipation is a thing of the future." Just before leaving France, he wrote as follows in acknowledging the receipt of the degree of Doctorate of Laws from Harvard University : "We have spent the prime of our lives in procuring them (the youth of the country) the precious blessing of liberty. Let them spend theirs in showing that it is the great parent of *science* and of virtue." Jefferson, when at liberty to give his personal interests free range, was much less limited than some of the quotations given above might suggest. The quotations, taken in their full context, are not so much evidence of his personal taste as of what he thought was the immediate need of a new nation occupying a new and still physically unconquered country. If his *acting* principle had been expressed, it would have been : "Necessities first ; luxuries in their due season."

Just as it was the "people" in whom he trusted as the foundation and ultimate security of self-governing institutions, so it was the enlightenment of the people as a whole which was his aim in promoting the advance of science. In a letter to a French friend, in which he says that his prayers are offered for the wellbeing

of France, he adds that her future government depends
not on "the state of science, no matter how exalted it
may be in a select band of enlightened men, but on the
condition of the general mind." What is hinted at in
these remarks is openly stated in other letters. As the
French Revolution went on from its beginnings, which
aroused his deepest sympathies, until there followed
the despotism and wars of Napoleon, he became increasingly skeptical of the social influence of a small
band of enlightened men — like the French *philosophes*.
His most extreme reaction is found in a letter to John
Adams : "As for France and England, with all their
preeminence in science, the one is a den of robbers,
and the other of pirates. And if science produces no
better fruits than tyranny, murder, rapine and destitu-
tion of national morality, I should wish our country
to be ignorant, honest and estimable, as our neighbor-
ing savages are." A more temperate statement of the
response evoked in him is found in a letter written in
1811 in which he acknowledged the receipt of a history
of the French Revolution. "Is reason to be forever
amused with the *hochets* of physical science, in which
she is indulged merely to divert her from solid speculations on the rights of man and wrongs of his oppressors
— it is impossible." At the same time, in speaking of
freedom, he throws in the phrase "the first born daughter of science." Jefferson's emphasis upon the relation
of science and learning to practical serviceability had
two sources. One of them was the newness of his
own country, and his conviction that needs should be
satisfied in the degree of their urgency. Political liberty — or, as he calls it in one place, physical liberty —
came first. A certain measure of material security
was needed to buttress this liberty. As these were
achieved, he was confident that the spread of education
and general enlightenment would add what was lacking
in the refinements of culture, things very precious to

him personally. Jefferson was a child of both the pioneer frontier and of the enlightenment of the 18th century — that century which he and John Adams regarded as the inauguration of a new era in human affairs.

The other cause of Jefferson's subordination of science and arts to social utility was his European experience. Science, no matter how "exalted," did not prevent wholesale misery and oppression if it was confined to a few. In spite of his very enjoyable personal relations with the leading intellectuals of Paris, his deepest sympathies went to the downtrodden masses whose huts he visited and whose food he ate. His affection for the "people" whose welfare was the real and final object of all social institutions and his faith in the "will of the people" as the basis of all legitimate political arrangements made him increasingly skeptical of advances in knowledge and the arts that left the mass of the people in a state of misery and degradation.

The balanced relation in Jefferson's ideas between the wellbeing of the masses and the higher cultivation of the arts and sciences is best expressed in his educational project. Elementary popular schooling educated the many. But it also served a selective purpose. It enabled the abler students to be picked out and to continue instruction in the middle grade. Through the agency of the latter the "natural aristocracy" of intellect and character would be selected who would go on to university education. State Universities have carried forward Jefferson's idea of a continuous educational ladder, that of Michigan being directly influenced by him. But in some respects, the plan is still in advance of what has been accomplished.

Jefferson's stay in France gave rise to the notion that his political philosophy was framed under French intellectual influence. It is easy to understand why, after the reaction produced by the excesses of the

Revolution, Jefferson's political enemies put forward
the idea as an accusation, extremists calling him a par-
ticipant in Gallic atheism, licentiousness and anarchy.
Just why scholars have entertained the same idea, not
as a charge against him, but as evidence of close intellectual relations between American social theory and
the French Enlightenment is not so clear. Every one
of Jefferson's characteristic political ideas (with one
possible exception) was definitely formulated by him
before he went to France. It is probable that his in-
clination toward the moral ideas of Epicurus, among
the classic writers, dates from acquaintance made in
Paris, but that did not affect his political ideas or even
his working ethical views. Rousseau is not even mentioned by him. The moderate French Charter of
Rights — a practical not a theoretical document — receives fairly extensive notice ; the Rights of Man the
barest casual mention.

The fact is — as selections in the text show clearly —
in Jefferson's opinion the movement, intellectual and
practical, was from the United States to France and
Europe, not from the latter to America. The possible
exception, alluded to above, is found in Jefferson's emphasis upon the moral inability of one generation to
bind a succeeding generation by imposing either a debt
or an unalterable constitution upon it. His assertion
that the "earth belongs in usufruct to the living ; that
the dead have neither powers nor rights over it" was
general in scope. But his argument (in a letter written from Paris) closes with a statement of the importance of the matter "in every country and most
especially in France." For, as he saw, if the new government could not abolish the laws regulating descent
of land, recover lands previously given to the Church,
abolish feudal and ecclesiastical special privileges, and
all perpetual monopolies, reformation of government
would be hamstrung before it got started.

The genuine and undeniable influence of France upon Jefferson is shown in a letter he wrote expressing his amazement upon finding the prevalence of monarchical ideas upon his return to New York, when, as he says, "fresh from France, while in its first and pure stage," he was "somewhat *whetted up* in my own republican principles." The real significance of the question of French influence upon him is found in a larger matter. The text which follows quotes at some length what Jefferson had to say about the sources of the ideas he expressed in the Declaration of Independence. I do not believe his remarks are intended, in their denial of indebtedness to this and to that writer, to set up a claim for originality. On the contrary, I believe his statement is to be taken literally that his purpose was simply to be "an expression of the American mind in words so firm and plain as to command assent." There was nothing that was novel in the idea that "governments derive their just powers from the consent of the governed," nor did it find its origin in Locke's writings — "nearly perfect" as were the latter in Jefferson's opinion. Even the right of the people "to alter or abolish" a government when it became destructive of the inherent moral rights of the governed had behind it a tradition that long antedated the writings of even Locke.

There was, nevertheless, something distinctive, something original, in the Declaration. It was not, however, in ideas at least as old as Aristotle and Cicero, the civil law was expounded by Pufendorf and others, and the political philosophy of the Fathers of the Church. What was new and significant was that these ideas were now set forth as an expression of the "American mind" that the American will was prepared to *act* upon. Jefferson was as profoundly convinced of the novelty of the *action* as a practical "experiment" — favorite word of his in connection with the institution of self-government — as he was of the orthodox character of the ideas as mere theory. The novelty of the practical attempt was, indeed, only set out in higher relief by the lack of novelty in underlying principles.

Jefferson used the language of the time in his assertion of "natural rights" upon which governments are based and which they must observe if they are to have legitimate authority. What is not now so plain is that the word *moral* can be substituted for the word *natural* whenever Jefferson used the latter in connection with law and rights, not only without changing his meaning but making it clearer to a modern reader. Not only does he say : "I am convinced man has no natural right in opposition to his social duties," and that "man was destined for society," but also that "questions of natural right are triable by their conformity with the moral sense and reason of man." In his letter to his French friend de Nemours, Jefferson develops his moral and political philosophy at some length by making a distinction "between the structure of the government and the moral principles" on which its administration is based. It is here that he says, "We of the United States are constitutionally and conscientiously democrats," and then goes on to give the statement a moral interpretation. Man is created with a want for society and with the powers to satisfy that want in concurrence with others. When he has procured that satisfaction by institution of a society, the latter is a product which man has a right to regulate "jointly with all those who have concurred in its procurement." "There exists a right independent of force" and "Justice is the fundamental law of society."

So much for the moral foundation and aim of government. Its structure concerns the special way in which men jointly exercise their right of control. He knew too much history and had had a share in making too much history not to know that governments have to be accommodated to the manners and habits of the people who compose a given state. When a population is large and spread over considerable space, it is not possible for a society to govern itself directly. It does so indirectly by representatives of its own choosing ; by those to whom it delegates its powers. "Governments are *more or less* republican as they have more or less of the element of popular election and control in their composition." Writing in 1816, he said that the United States, measured by this criterion, were less republican than they should be, a lack he attributed to the fact that the lawmakers who came from large cities had learned to be afraid of the populace, and then unjustly extended their fears to the "independent, the happy and therefore orderly citizens of the United States." Any one who starts from the just mentioned moral principle of Jefferson as a premise and adds to it as another premise the principle that the only legitimate "object of the institution of government is to secure the greatest degree of happiness possible to the general mass of those associated under it" can, with little trouble, derive the further tenets of Jefferson's political creed.

The will of the people as the moral basis of government and the happiness of the people as its controlling aim were so firmly established with Jefferson that it was axiomatic that the only alternative to the republican position was fear, in lieu of trust, of the people. Given fear of them, it followed, as by mathematical necessity, not only that they must *not* be given a large share in the conduct of government, but that they must themselves be controlled by force, moral or physical or both, and by appeal to some special interest served by government — an appeal which, according to Jefferson, inevitably meant the use of means to corrupt the people. Jefferson's trust in the people was a faith in what he sometimes called their common sense and sometimes their reason. They might be fooled and misled for a time, but give them light and in the long run their oscillations this way and that will describe what in effect is a straight course ahead.

I am not underestimating Jefferson's abilities as a practical politician when I say that this deep-seated faith in the people and their responsiveness to enlightenment properly presented was a most important factor in enabling him to effect, against great odds, "the revolution of 1800." It is the cardinal element bequeathed by Jefferson to the American tradition.

Jefferson's belief in the necessity for strict limitation of the powers of officials had both a general and a special or historic source. As for the latter, had not the Revolution itself been fought because of the usurpation of power by the officers of a government? And were not the political opponents of Republicanism, in Jefferson's opinion, men so moved by admiration of the British constitution that they wished to establish a "strong" government in this country, one not above the use of methods of corruption — not indeed as an end in itself but as a means of procuring the allegiance of the populace more effectively and in a less costly way than by use of direct coercion? On general principles, Jefferson knew that possession of unusual and irresponsible power corrupts those who wield it; that officials are, after all, human beings affected by ordinary weaknesses of human nature, "wares from the same workshop, made of the same materials." Hence they were to be continually watched, tested and checked, as well as constitutionally limited in their original grant of powers.

There are, however, two important points in which popular representations of Jeffersonian democracy are often at fault. One of them concerns the basic importance of the will of the people in relation to the law-making power, constitutional and ordinary. There is

no doubt that Jefferson was strongly in favor of speci-
fying in the constitution the powers that could be exercised by officials, executive, legislative and judicial,
and then holding them, by strict construction, to the
powers specified. But he also believed that "every
people have their own particular habits, ways of thinking, manners, etc., which have grown up with them
from their infancy, are become a part of their nature,
and to which the regulations which are to make them
happy must be accommodated." As he states the
principle elsewhere · "The excellence of every government is its adaptation to the state of those to be governed by it." In this matter, especially, Jefferson's
theories were tempered by practical experience.

His idealism was a moral idealism, not a dreamy
utopianism. He was aware that conclusions drawn
from the past history of mankind were against the success of the experiment that was being tried on American soil. He was quite sure that Latin American
countries would succeed in throwing off the yoke of
Spain and Portugal, but he was decidedly skeptical
about their capacity for self-government, and feared
their future was one of a succession of military despot-
isms for a long time to come. He was conscious that
chances for greater success of the experiment in the
United States were dependent upon events which
might be regarded either as fortunate accidents or as
providential dispensations : the wide ocean protecting
the country from oppressive governments in Europe ;
the "Anglo-Saxon" tradition of liberties ; even the jealousies of religious denominations that prevented the
State Establishment of any one church, and hence
worked for religious liberty ; the immense amount of
free land and available natural sources with consequent
continual freedom of movement ; the independence
and vigor that were bred on the frontier, etc. Even
so, he had fears for the future when the country should

be urbanized and industrialized, though upon the whole, he says, he tended by temperament to take counsel of his hopes rather than his fears.

In direct line with his conviction on this point was his belief in the necessity of periodic revisions of the constitution, one to take place every twenty years, and his belief that the process of ordinary amendment had been made too difficult. His faith in the right of the people to govern themselves in their own way and in their ability to exercise the right wisely — provided they were enlightened by education and by free discussion — was stronger than his faith in any article of his own political creed — except this one. His own convictions as to the proper forms of government were strong, and he contended ably for their realization. But he was conciliatory by temperament and by practical policy. Students and historians have criticized him for not trying harder to put into effect after the "revolution of 1800" the reforms he had been urging before that time, especially as he based his opposition to Adams upon their absence. Doubtless he was moved by considerations of political expediency. But there is also no reason to doubt the sincerity of those expressions of his which set forth his willingness to subordinate his own political policies to the judgment of the people. Trust in the popular will was temperamental, constitutional with him.

In any case, he was no friend of what he called "sanctimonious reverence" for the constitution. He adhered to the view, expressed in the Declaration of Independence, that people are more disposed to suffer evils than to right them by abolishing forms to which they are accustomed. It was the more important, accordingly, to recognize that "laws and institution must go hand in hand with the progress of the human mind" and that institutions must change with change of circumstances brought about by "discoveries, new truths, change of opinions and manners." Were he alive, he would note and scourge that lack of democratic faith which, in the professed name of democracy, asserts that the "ark of the covenant is too sacred to be touched." Jefferson saw that periodical overhauling of the fundamental law was the alternative to change effected only by violence and repetition of the old historic round "of oppressions, rebellions, reformations, oppressions. . ." There was but one thing which was unchangeable, and that was the "inherent and inalienable rights of man."

The other point in which Jefferson's ideas have not been adequately represented has to do with his belief that state governments "are the true barriers of our liberty"; and his fear of centralized government at Washington: — not that he did not have the belief and the fear, and hold them with strong conviction, but that the ideas with which he supplemented them have not received due attention. In the main text which follows there are selections, of considerable extent, which show the importance he attached to self-governing communities of much smaller size than the state or even the county. He was impressed, practically as well as theoretically, with the effectiveness of the New England town meeting, and wished to see something of the sort made an organic part of the governing process of the whole country. Division of every county into wards was first suggested by him in connection with organization of an elementary school system. But even from his early service in the legislature of Virginia to the latest years of his life he urged his plan and expressed the hope that while it had not been adopted, it would be at some time. In a letter written after he had reached the age of three score years and ten, he says: "As Cato concluded every speech with the words 'Carthago delenda est' so do I every opinion, with the injunction, 'Divide the coun-

ties into wards,' " referring in 1815 to a bill he had introduced forty years at least before, at the time when
his other bills for abolition of entails in land and of
primogeniture were adopted.

While the first aim of the division into small local
units was the establishment and care of popular elementary schools, their purpose extended, in the mind
of Jefferson, far beyond that function.   The aim was
to make the wards "little republics, with a warden at
the head of each, for all those concerns, which being
under their eye, they would better manage than the
larger republics of the county or State."   They were
to have the "care of the poor, roads, police, elections,
nomination of jurors, administration of justice in small
cases, elementary exercises of militia."   In short, they
were to exercise directly with respect to their own
affairs all the functions of government, civil and military.   In addition, when any important wider matter
came up for decision, all wards would be called into
meetings on the same day, so that the collective sense
of the whole people would be produced.   The plan
was not adopted.   But it was an essential part of Jefferson's political philosophy.   The significance of the
doctrine of "states rights" as he held it, is incomplete
both theoretically and practically until this plan is taken
into the reckoning.   "The elementary republics of the
wards, the county republics, the State republics and the
Republic of the Union would form a gradation of
authorities."   Every man would then share in the government of affairs not merely on election day but every
day.   In a letter to John Adams, written in 1813, he
says he still has great hope that the plan will be
adopted, as it then will form "the keystone of the arch
of our government."   It is for this reason that I say
this view of self-government is very inadequately represented in the usual form in which it is set forth —
as a glorification of state against federal governments,

and still more as a theoretical opposition to all government save as a necessary evil. The heart of his philosophy of politics is found in his effort to institute these small administrative and legislative units as the keystone of the arch.

As was suggested earlier, the essentially moral nature of Jefferson's political philosophy is concealed from us at the present time because of the change that has taken place in the language in which moral ideas are expressed. The "self-evident truths" about the equality of all men by creation and the existence of "inherent and inalienable rights," * appear today to have a legal rather than a moral meaning ; and in addition, the intellectual basis of the legal theory of natural law and natural rights has been undermined by historical and philosophical criticism. In Jefferson's own mind, the words had a definitely ethical import, intimately and vitally connected with his view of God and Nature. The latter connection comes out more clearly if possible in the Preamble, in which he refers to the necessity of the American people taking the "separate and equal station to which the laws of nature and of nature's God entitle them."

These phrases were not rhetorical flourishes nor were they accommodated for reasons of expediency to what Jefferson thought would be popular with the people of the country. Jefferson was a sincere theist. Although his rejection of supernaturalism and of the authority of churches and their creeds caused him to be denounced as an atheist, he was convinced, beyond any peradventure, on *natural* and rational grounds of the existence of a divine righteous Creator who manifested his purposes in the structure of the world, espe-

* "Certain" was substituted for "inherent" by the Congress. The first manuscript draft, later changed by Jefferson himself, read that "all men are created equal and independent ; that from that equal creation they derive rights."

theological dimension to nature - freedom

cially in that of society and the human conscience. The natural equality of all human beings was not psychological nor legal. It was intrinsically moral, as a consequence of the equal *moral* relation all human beings sustain to their Creator ; — equality of moral claims and of moral responsibilities. Positive law — or municipal law, as Jefferson termed it — and political institutions thus have both a moral foundation and a moral criterion or measure.

The word "faith" is thus applied advisedly to the attitude of Jefferson toward the people's will, and its right to control political institutions and policies. The faith had a genuinely religious quality. The forms of government and law, even of the Constitution, might and should change. But the inherent and inalienable rights of man were unchangeable, because they express the will of the righteous creator of man embodied in the very structure of society and conscience. Jefferson was not an "individualist" in the sense of the British laissez-faire liberal school. Individual human beings receive the right of self-government "with their being from the hand of nature." As an eighteenth century deist and believer in natural religion, Jefferson connected Nature and Nature's God inseparably in his thought. He writes that he has "no fear but that the result of our experiment will be that men may be trusted to govern themselves without a master. Could the contrary of this be proved, I should conclude either that there is no God, or that he is a malevolent being." These words are to be taken literally not rhetorically, if one wishes to understand Jefferson's democratic faith. He even engages in construction of the following syllogism. "Man was created for social intercourse ; but social intercourse cannot be maintained without a sense of justice ; then man must have been created with a sense of justice." The connection of justice — or equity — with equality of rights and duties

was a commonplace of the moral tradition of Christen-
dom. Jefferson took the tradition seriously. The
statements of Jefferson about the origin of the Declaration of Independence, statements already quoted,
are confirmed in what he wrote shortly before his
death. "We had no occasion to search into musty
records, to hunt up royal parchments, or to investigate
the laws and institutions of a semi-barbarous ancestry.
We appealed to those of nature, and found them engraved on our hearts."

Other days bring other words and other opinions
behind words that are used. The terms in which Jefferson expressed his belief in the moral criterion for
judging all political arrangements and his belief that
republican institutions are the only ones that are morally legitimate are not now current. It is doubtful,
however, whether defense of democracy against the
attacks to which it is subjected does not depend upon
taking once more the position Jefferson took about its
moral basis and purpose, even though we have to find
another set of words in which to formulate the moral
ideal served by democracy. A renewal of faith in
common human nature, in its potentialities in general
and in its power in particular to respond to reason
and truth, is a surer bulwark against totalitarianism
than is demonstration of material success or devout
worship of special legal and political forms.

Jefferson wrote no set treatises. In reply to a suggestion that he write a history of his own times, he
replied that "while in public life I had not the time,
and now that I am retired I am past the time." He
probably would have made a similar reply, couched
in even more emphatic terms, to a suggestion that he
write a book on the principles of government. He
would have been content to point to the record of his
activities. But he was an indefatigable letter writer.

In a letter written after he was seventy years of age, he says he engages in correspondence till noon every day, some days from sunrise to one or two o'clock. In his eightieth year he reports that having counted the letters in his file of the previous year, he found they amounted to 1267, "many requiring answers of elaborate research." The published letters of the first month of 1816 add up to over 12,000 words. It is from these letters and his public documents that the material of the following pages is drawn. I believe they make up in actuality and in sincerity what is lacking in system. The problem of selection was easier to solve than that of arrangement, since it is clear that there is no preordained logical arrangement for the materials of a correspondence that extends over a period of sixty active and full years. Many schemes of arrangement suggest themselves. I have been guided chiefly by a desire to combine the more theoretical statements with passages recording his own observations, and illustrate thereby that union of principle and practice which seems to me to constitute the greatness of Jefferson.

* * *

Jefferson's life was peculiarly divided, almost split, between his public career and his private and domestic activities. It is probably owing to something pretty fundamental in his own character that for the most part he preferred to permit the former to speak for itself, and that, when questioned about the latter, he said they were substantially similar to those of any other American citizen of the time. Consequently, in spite of the autobiographical notes which he wrote, there is curiously little material available of a strictly personal kind. We know he was a cultivated gentleman, of personal charm. That he was of handsome physique is proved by the portraits painted of him by

Stuart, Peale, Desnoyers, Sully, and by the statues of Powers and D'Angers. Strongly opposed to extravagance and debt in public affairs, he was never out of debt himself. He must have spent several small fortunes in building, tearing down, and rebuilding his home at Monticello and experimenting with the buildings for the University of Virginia, whose architect and supervisor he was, down to personally deciding by chemical experiment the composition of the cement used in laying the brick walls.

His father was a pioneer frontiersman, one of the first three or four to venture to what was at that time the western limit of settlement in the Virginia territory, a man with slight opportunity for schooling and yet so "eager after information" and so bent on improvement that he made of himself a skilled surveyor who, in company with a professor of mathematics, fixed the boundary line between Virginia and North Carolina, and who insisted upon giving his son the best classical education attainable at that time in America. Doubtless it was from him and from the pioneer environment in which men were compelled to be jacks-of-all-trades that Thomas Jefferson derived his lifelong interest in all mechanical inventions and gadgets, and his abiding respect for personal industry and handicraft. His respect for labor is expressed in a letter he wrote to a friend in France when, upon his return from that country, he found that the deranged state of his farms required him to find a new source of revenue : "My new trade of nailmaking is to me in this country what an additional title of nobility or the ensigns of a new order are in Europe." It is not unduly speculative to suppose that it was from his frontier experience that he also derived that sense of the inevitable continental expansion of the United States which seems to have marked him alone among the statesmen of the time, and which later expressed itself

in the Louisiana purchase and in his attitude toward
Florida and even Cuba.

We know that Jefferson married, when approach-
ing the age of thirty, a widow twenty-three years old,
the daughter of a successful local lawyer ; that for ten
years before her death they lived in great happiness,
and that Jefferson never remarried. But again it seems
characteristic of the sharp line drawn by Jefferson between his public career and his private life that he left
little record of her and his life with her, save a statement in a letter to a French friend that having "rested
all prospects of future happiness on domestic and lit-
erary objects, a single event wiped away my plans and
left me a blank." This blank, caused by his wife's death,
he intimates to be the main reason why he was willing
to accept his appointment as Ambassador to France,
to succeed, but *not*, as he always said, to "replace"
Benjamin Franklin, "The greatest man and ornament
of the age and country in which he lived." During
the ten years of married life, five daughters and one
son were born to them. The son lived less than a
month ; the husbands of two of his daughters were
among the closest of Jefferson's correspondents, but
even with them ideas and public affairs are discussed
rather than intimate personal and family matters.

The combination in Jefferson of a kind of objective
pride in his public career and a frequently expressed
preference for a life of retirement devoted to management of his estate, to reading and writing, to making
scientific observations and studies, and to domestic
happiness, finds expression in his replies to correspondents who asked him for material for a biography.   The
uniform tenor of his response is that "The only exact
testimony of a man is his actions" and of these others
must be left to be the judge. Aside from his public
activities, there was nothing in his life worthy of spe-

cial record. After his fame was firmly established he even refused to state the date of his birth on the ground that the only birthday he wished to have recognized was "that of my country's liberties."

The combination of reserve and dislike for public office with extraordinary skill and success as a practical politician laid Jefferson open to the charge of inconsistency and even insincerity. Such charges are impossible either to support or to refute long after the events which occurred, and are unprofitable. That Jefferson disliked controversy and was disposed to be conciliatory and compromising there is, however, no reason to doubt. The exceptions made in the case of Hamilton and to a lesser degree in that of Chief Justice Marshall are of the kind that prove a rule. The latter is exemplified in the pain he felt at the break with John Adams and the great joy he experienced in the restoration of friendly relations. What he said about the conduct of Franklin at the French Court might almost be taken as defense of charges sometimes brought against himself: "His temper was so amiable and conciliatory, his conduct so rational, never urging impossibilities, so moderate and attentive to the difficulties of others, that what his enemies called subserviency, I saw was only a reasonable disposition," — not that he was charged with subserviency, but with inconsistency between professed principles and actual behavior. In any case, if Jefferson is better known for his political ideas and his public acts than as a human being, it is just what he would have wished for himself. Considering his times and the difficult and important part he played in them, there remains the image of a magnanimous, high-spirited public gentleman who subordinated himself with complete devotion to what he conceived to be the welfare of the country he loved. I do not see how any one can doubt that he was careless of his own future fame when that was put in comparison with the future of the democratic ideas he served, nor that, on the other hand, he felt sure of his own reputation as long as those ideas were safe.

POLITICAL PHILOSOPHY

When, in the course of human events, it becomes necessary for one people to dissolve the political bands which have connected them with another, and to assume among the powers of the earth the separate and equal station to which the laws of nature and of nature's God entitle them, a decent respect to the opinions of mankind requires that they should declare the causes which impel them to the separation.

We hold these truths to be self evident : that all men are created equal ; that they are endowed by their creator with [*inherent and*] inalienable rights ; that among these are life, liberty, and the pursuit of happiness ; that to secure these rights, governments are instituted among men, deriving their just powers from the consent of the governed ; that whenever any form of government becomes destructive of these ends, it is the right of the people to alter or to abolish it, and to institute new government, laying its foundation on such principles, and organizing its powers in such form, as to them shall seem most likely to effect their safety and happiness.

* * *

With respect to our rights, and the acts of the British government contravening those rights, there was but one opinion on this side of the water. All American whigs thought alike on these subjects. When forced, therefore, to resort to arms for redress, an appeal to the tribunal of the world was deemed proper for our justification. This was the object of the Declaration of Independence. Not to find out new principles, or new arguments, never before thought of, not merely to say things which had never been said before ;

but to place before mankind the common sense of the
subject, in terms so plain and firm as to command their
assent, and to justify ourselves in the independent stand
we are compelled to take. Neither aiming at originality of principle or sentiment, nor yet copied from
any particular and previous writing, it was intended to
be an expression of the American mind, and to give to
that expression the proper tone and spirit called for by
the occasion. All its authority rests then on the har-
monizing sentiments of the day, whether expressed in
conversation, in letters, printed essays, or in the elementary books of public right, as Aristotle, Cicero,
Locke, Sidney, &c. Pickering's observations, and Mr.
Adams' in addition, "that it contained no new ideas,
that it is a common-place compilation, its sentiments
hacknied in Congress for two years before, and its
essence contained in Otis' pamphlet," may all be true.
Of that I am not to be the judge. I know only that
I turned to neither book nor pamphlet while writing
it. I did not consider it as any part of my charge to
invent new ideas altogether, and to offer no sentiment
which had ever been expressed before.

* * *

By way of anticipation, I shall make to you * a profession of my political faith ; in confidence that you will
consider every future imputation on me of a contrary
complexion, as bearing on its front the mark of falsehood and calumny.

I do then, with sincere zeal, wish an inviolable preservation of our present federal Constitution, according
to the true sense in which it was adopted by the States,
that in which it was advocated by its friends, and not
that which its enemies apprehended, who therefore
became its enemies ; and I am opposed to the monarch-
ising its features by the forms of its administration,

* Elbridge Gerry.

with a view to conciliate a first transition to a President
and Senate for life, and from that to an hereditary tenure of these offices, and thus to worm out the elective
principle. I am for preserving to the States the powers
not yielded by them to the Union, and to the legislature of the Union its constitutional share in the division of powers; and I am not for transferring all the
powers of the States to the General Government, and
all those of that government to the executive branch.
I am for a government rigorously frugal and simple,
applying all the possible savings of the public revenue
to the discharge of the national debt; and not for a
multiplication of officers and salaries merely to make
partisans, and for increasing, by every device, the public debt, on the principle of its being a public blessing.
I am for relying, for internal defence, on our militia
solely, till actual invasion, and for such a naval force
only as may protect our coasts and harbors from such
depredations as we have experienced; and not for a
standing army in time of peace, which may overawe
the public sentiment; nor for a navy, which, by its
own expenses and the eternal wars in which it will im-
plicate us, will grind us with public burthens, and sink
us under them. I am for free commerce with all nations; political connection with none; and little or no
diplomatic establishment. And I am not for linking
ourselves by new treaties with the quarrels of Europe;
entering that field of slaughter to preserve their balance, or joining in the confederacy of kings to war
against the principles of liberty. I am for freedom of
religion, and against all maneuvres to bring about a
legal ascendancy of one sect over another: for freedom of the press, and against all violations of the Constitution to silence by force and not by reason the
complaints or criticisms, just or unjust, of our citizens
against the conduct of their agents. And I am for encouraging the progress of science in all its branches;

and not for raising a hue and cry against the sacred name of philosophy ; for awing the human mind by stories of raw-head and bloody bones to a distrust of its own vision, and to repose implicitly on that of others ; to go backwards instead of forwards to look for improvements ; to believe that government, religion, morality, and every other science were in the highest perfection in ages of the darkest ignorance, and that nothing can ever be devised more perfect than what was established by our forefathers. To these I will add, that I was a sincere well-wisher to the success of the French revolution, and still wish it may end in the establishment of a free and well-ordered republic ; but I have not been insensible under the atrocious depredations they have committed on our commerce.

* * *

The fact is, that at the formation of our government, many had formed their political opinions on European writings and practices, believing the experience of old countries, and especially of England, abusive as it was, to be a safer guide than mere theory. The doctrines of Europe were, that men in numerous associations cannot be restrained within the limits of order and justice, but by forces physical and moral, wielded over them by authorities independent of their will. Hence their organization of kings, hereditary nobles, and priests. Still further to constrain the brute force of the people, they deem it necessary to keep them down by hard labor, poverty and ignorance, and to take from them, as from bees, so much of their earnings, as that unremitting labor shall be necessary to obtain a sufficient surplus barely to sustain a scanty and miserable life. Ours, on the contrary, was to maintain the will of the majority of the convention, and of the people themselves. We believed, with them, that man was a rational animal, endowed by nature with rights, and with an innate sense of justice ; and that he could be restrained from wrong and protected in right, by moderate powers, confided to persons of his own choice, and held to their duties by dependence on his own will. We believed that the complicated organization of kings, nobles, and priests, was not the wisest nor best to effect the happiness of associated man ; that wisdom and virtue were not hereditary ; that the trappings of such a machinery, consumed by their expense, those earnings of industry, they were meant to protect, and, by the inequalities they produced, exposed liberty to sufferance. We believed that men, enjoying in ease and security the full fruits of their own industry, enlisted by all their interests on the side of law and order, habituated to think for themselves, and to follow their reason as their guide, would be more easily and safely governed, than with minds nourished in error, and vitiated and debased, as in Europe, by ignorance, indigence and oppression. The cherishment of the people then was our principle, the fear and distrust of them, that of the other party. Composed, as we were, of the landed and laboring interests of the country, we could not be less anxious for a government of law and order than were the inhabitants of the cities, the strongholds of federalism. And whether our efforts to save the principles and form of our constitution have not been salutary, let the present republican freedom, order and prosperity of our country determine.

* * *

Our Revolution commenced on more favorable ground. It presented us an album on which we were free to write what we pleased. We had no occasion to search into musty records, to hunt up royal parchments, or to investigate the laws and institutions of a semi-barbarous ancestry. We appealed to those of nature, and found them engraved on our hearts. Yet we did not avail ourselves of all the advantages of our position. We had never been permitted to exercise self-government. When forced to assume it, we were novices in its science. Its principles and forms had entered little into our former education. We established however some, although not all its important principles. The constitutions of most of our States assert, that all power is inherent in the people; that they may exercise it by themselves, in all cases to which they think themselves competent, (as in electing their functionaries executive and legislative, and deciding by a jury of themselves, in all judiciary cases in which any fact is involved,) or they may act by representatives, freely and equally chosen; that it is their right and duty to be at all times armed; that they are entitled to freedom of person, freedom of religion, freedom of property, and freedom of the press. In the structure of our legislatures, we think experience has proved the benefit of subjecting questions to two separate bodies of deliberants; but in constituting these, natural right has been mistaken, some making one of these bodies, and some both, the representatives of property instead of persons; whereas the double deliberation might be as well obtained without any violation of true principle, either by requiring a greater age in one of the bodies, or by electing a proper number of representatives of persons, dividing them by lots into two chambers, and renewing the division at frequent intervals, in order to break up all cabals. Virginia, of which I am myself a native and resident, was not only the first of the States, but, I believe I may say, the first of the nations of the earth, which assembled its wise men peaceably together to form a fundamental constitution, to commit it to writing, and place it among their archives, where every one should be free to appeal to its text. But this act was very imperfect. The other States, as they proceeded successively to the same work, made successive improvements; and several of them, still further corrected by experience, have, by conventions, still further amended their first forms. My own State has gone on so far with its *première ébauche* ; but it is now proposing to call a convention for amendment. Among other improvements, I hope they will adopt the subdivision of our counties into wards. Each ward would thus be a small republic within itself, and every man in the State would thus become an acting member of the common government, transacting in person a great portion of its rights and duties, subordinate indeed, yet important, and entirely within his competence. The wit of man cannot devise a more solid basis for a free, durable and well-administered republic.

To the State governments are reserved all legislation and administration, in affairs which concern their own citizens only, and to the federal government is given whatever concerns foreigners, or the citizens of other States ; these functions alone being made federal. The one is the domestic, the other the foreign branch of the same government ; neither having control over the other, but within its own department. There are one or two exceptions only to this partition of power. But, you * may ask, if the two departments should claim each the same subject of power, where is the common umpire to decide ultimately between them ? In cases of little importance or urgency, the prudence of both parties will keep them aloof from the questionable ground ; but if it can neither be avoided nor compromised, a convention of the States must be called, to ascribe the doubtful power to that department which they may think best.

* * *

During the contest of opinion through which we have passed, the animation of discussion and of exertions has sometimes worn an aspect which might im-

* Major John Cartwright.

pose on strangers unused to think freely and to speak
and to write what they think ; but this being now decided by the voice of the nation, announced according
to the rules of the constitution, all will, of course, ar-
range themselves under the will of the law, and unite
in common efforts for the common good. All, too,
will bear in mind this sacred principle, that though the
will of the majority is in all cases to prevail, that will,
to be rightful, must be reasonable ; that the minority
possess their equal rights, which equal laws must protect, and to violate which would be oppression. Let
us, then, fellow citizens, unite with one heart and one
mind. Let us restore to social intercourse that har-
mony and affection without which liberty and even life
itself are but dreary things. And let us reflect that
having banished from our land that religious intolerance under which mankind so long bled and suffered,
we have yet gained little if we countenance a political
intolerance as despotic, as wicked, and capable of as
bitter and bloody persecutions. We have called by
different names brethren of the same principle. We
are all republicans — we are federalists. If there be
any among us who would wish to dissolve this Union
or to change its republican form, let them stand un-
disturbed as monuments of the safety with which error
of opinion may be tolerated where reason is left free to
combat it. I know, indeed, that some honest men fear
that a republican government cannot be strong ; that
this government is not strong enough. But would the
honest patriot, in the full tide of successful experiment, abandon a government which has so far kept us
free and firm, on the theoretic and visionary fear that
this government, the world's best hope, may by possibility want energy to preserve itself ? I trust not.
I believe this, on the contrary, the strongest government on earth. I believe it is the only one where
every man, at the call of the laws, would fly to the

standard of the law, and would meet invasions of the public order as his own personal concern. Sometimes it is said that man cannot be trusted with the government of himself. Can he, then, be trusted with the government of others? Or have we found angels in the forms of kings to govern him? Let history answer this question.

It is proper that you * should understand what I deem the essential principles of our government, and consequently those which ought to shape its administration. I will compress them within the narrowest compass they will bear, stating the general principle, but not all its limitations. Equal and exact justice to all men, of whatever state or persuasion, religious or political; peace, commerce, and honest friendship, with all nations — entangling alliances with none; the support of the state governments in all their rights, as the most competent administrations for our domestic concerns and the surest bulwarks against anti-republican tendencies; the preservation of the general government in its whole constitutional vigor, as the sheet anchor of our peace at home and safety abroad; a jealous care of the right of election by the people — a mild and safe corrective of abuses which are lopped by the sword of the revolution where peaceable remedies are unprovided; absolute acquiescence in the decisions of the majority — the vital principle of republics, from which there is no appeal but to force, the vital principle and immediate parent of despotism; a well-disciplined militia — our best reliance in peace and for the first moments of war, till regulars may relieve them; the supremacy of the civil over the military authority; economy in the public expense, that labor may be lightly burdened; the honest payment of our debts and sacred preservation of the public faith; encouragement of agriculture, and of commerce as its handmaid;

* The citizens of the United States of America.

the diffusion of information and the arraignment of all
abuses at the bar of public reason ; freedom of religion ;
freedom of the press ; freedom of person under the
protection of the *habeas corpus* ; and trial by juries im-
partially selected — these principles form the bright
constellation which has gone before us, and guided
our steps through an age of revolution and reformation. The wisdom of our sages and the blood of our
heroes have been devoted to their attainment. They
should be the creed of our political faith — the text of
civil instruction — the touchstone by which to try the
services of those we trust ; and should we wander from
them in moments of error or alarm, let us hasten to
retrace our steps and to regain the road which alone
leads to peace, liberty, and safety.

* * *

In every government on earth is some trace of human weakness, some germ of corruption and degeneracy, which cunning will discover, and wickedness
insensibly open, cultivate and improve. Every government degenerates when trusted to the rulers of the
people alone. The people themselves therefore are its
only safe depositories. And to render them safe, their
minds must be improved to a certain degree. This indeed is not all that is necessary, though it be essentially
necessary. An amendment of our constitution must
here come in aid of the public education. The influence over government must be shared among all the
people. If every individual which composes their mass
participates of the ultimate authority, the government
will be safe ; because the corrupting the whole mass
will exceed any private resources of wealth ; and public
ones cannot be provided but by levies on the people.
In this case every man would have to pay his own
price. The government of Great Britain has been cor-
rupted, because but one man in ten has a right to vote

for members of parliament. The sellers of the government, therefore, get nine-tenths of their price clear. It has been thought that corruption is restrained by confining the right of suffrage to a few of the wealthier of the people ; but it would be more effectually restrained by an extension of that right to such numbers as would bid defiance to the means of corruption.

* * *

Distinguishing between the structure of the government and the moral principles on which you * prescribe its administration, with the latter we concur cordially, with the former we should not. We of the United States, you know, are constitutionally and conscientiously democrats. We consider society as one of the natural wants with which man has been created ; that he has been endowed with faculties and qualities to effect its satisfaction by concurrence of others having the same want ; that when, by the exercise of these faculties, he has procured a state of society, it is one of his acquisitions which he has a right to regulate and control, jointly indeed with all those who have concurred in the procurement, whom he cannot exclude from its use or direction more than they him. We think experience has proved it safer, for the mass of individuals composing the society, to reserve to themselves personally the exercise of all rightful powers to which they are competent, and to delegate those to which they are not competent to deputies named, and removable for unfaithful conduct, by themselves immediately. Hence, with us, the people (by which is meant the mass of individuals composing the society) being competent to judge of the facts occurring in ordinary life, they have retained the functions of judges of facts, under the name of jurors ; but being unqualified for the management of affairs requiring

* M. Dupont de Nemours.

intelligence above the common level, yet competent judges of human character, they chose, for their management, representatives, some by themselves immediately, others by electors chosen by themselves.

I acknowledge myself strong in affection to our own form, yet both of us act and think from the same motive, we both consider the people as our children, and love them with parental affection. But you love them as infants whom you are afraid to trust without nurses ; and I as adults whom I freely leave to self-government.

* * *

No, my friend,* the way to have good and safe government, is not to trust it all to one, but to divide it among the many, distributing to every one exactly the functions he is competent to. Let the national government be entrusted with the defence of the nation, and its foreign and federal relations ; the State governments with the civil rights, laws, police, and administration of what concerns the State generally ; the counties with the local concerns of the counties, and each ward direct the interests within itself. It is by dividing and subdividing these republics from the great national one down through all its subordinations, until it ends in the administration of every man's farm by himself ; by placing under every one what his own eye may superintend, that all will be done for the best. What has destroyed liberty and the rights of man in every government which has ever existed under the sun ? The generalizing and concentrating all cares and powers into one body, no matter whether of the autocrats of Russia or France, or of the aristocrats of a Venetian senate. And I do believe that if the Almighty has not decreed that man shall never be free, (and it is a blasphemy to believe it,) that the secret will be found to be in the making himself the deposi-

* Joseph C. Cabell.

tory of the powers respecting himself, so far as he is competent to them, and delegating only what is beyond his competence by a synthetical process, to higher and higher orders of functionaries, so as to trust fewer and fewer powers in proportion as the trustees become more and more oligarchical. The elementary republics of the wards, the county republics, the State republics, and the republic of the Union, would form a gradation of authorities, standing each on the basis of law, holding every one its delegated share of powers, and constituting truly a system of fundamental balances and checks for the government. Where every man is a sharer in the direction of his ward-republic, or of some of the higher ones, and feels that he is a participator in the government of affairs, not merely at an election one day in the year, but every day; when there shall not be a man in the State who will not be a member of some one of its councils, great or small, he will let the heart be torn out of his body sooner than his power be wrested from him by a Cæsar or a Bonaparte. How powerfully did we feel the energy of this organization in the case of embargo? I felt the foundations of the government shaken under my feet by the New England townships. There was not an individual in their States whose body was not thrown with all its momentum into action; and although the whole of the other States were known to be in favor of the measure, yet the organization of this little selfish minority enabled it to overrule the Union. What would the unwieldy counties of the middle, the south, and the west do? Call a county meeting, and the drunken loungers at and about the court houses would have collected, the distances being too great for the good people and the industrious generally to attend. The character of those who really met would have been the measure of the weight they would have had in the scale of public opinion. As Cato, then, concluded every speech with the words, "*Carthago delenda est*," so do I every opinion, with the injunction, "divide the counties into wards." Begin them only for a single purpose ; they will soon show for what others they are the best instruments.

But it is not by the consolidation, or concentration of powers, but by their distribution, that good government is effected. Were not this great country already divided into States, that division must be made, that each might do for itself what concerns itself directly, and what it can so much better do than a distant authority. Every State again is divided into counties, each to take care of what lies within its local bounds ; each county again into townships or wards, to manage minuter details ; and every ward into farms, to be governed each by its individual proprietor. Were we directed from Washington when to sow, and when to reap, we should soon want bread. It is by this partition of cares, descending in gradation from general to particular, that the mass of human affairs may be best managed, for the good and prosperity of all.

* * *

One may conclude too hastily, that nature has formed man insusceptible of any other government than that of force, a conclusion not founded in truth nor experience. Societies exist under three forms, sufficiently distinguishable. 1. Without government, as among our Indians. 2. Under governments, wherein the will of every one has a just influence ; as is the case in England, in a slight degree, and in our States, in a great one. 3. Under governments of force ; as is the case in all other monarchies, and in most of the other republics. To have an idea of the curse of existence under these last, they must be seen. It is a government of wolves over sheep. It is a problem, not clear in my mind, that the first condition is not the best.

But I believe it to be inconsistent with any great degree of population. The second state has a great deal of good in it. The mass of mankind under that, enjoys a precious degree of liberty and happiness. It has its evils, too ; the principal of which is the turbulence to which it is subject. But weigh this against the oppressions of monarchy, and it becomes nothing. *Malo periculosam libertatem quam quietam servitutem.* Even this evil is productive of good. It prevents the degeneracy of government, and nourishes a general attention to the public affairs. I hold it, that a little rebellion, now and then, is a good thing, and as necessary in the political world as storms in the physical. Unsuccessful rebellions, indeed, generally establish the encroachments on the rights of the people, which have produced them. An observation of this truth should render honest republican governors so mild in their punishment of rebellions, as not to discourage them too much. It is a medicine necessary for the sound health of government.

. . . And say,* finally, whether peace is best preserved by giving energy to the government, or information to the people. This last is the most certain, and the most legitimate engine of government. Educate and inform the whole mass of the people. Enable them to see that it is their interest to preserve peace and order, and they will preserve them. And it requires no very high degree of education to convince them of this. They are the only sure reliance for the preservation of our liberty. After all, it is my principle that the will of the majority should prevail. If they approve the proposed constitution in all its parts, I shall concur in it cheerfully, in hopes they will amend it, whenever they shall find it works wrong. This reliance cannot deceive us, as long as we remain virtuous ; and I think we shall be so, as long as agricul-

* James Madison.

ture is our principal object, which will be the case, while there remains vacant lands in any part of America. When we get piled upon one another in large cities, as in Europe, we shall become corrupt as in Europe, and go to eating one another as they do there.

* * *

We think, in America, that it is necessary to introduce the people into every department of government, as far as they are capable of exercising it ; and that this is the only way to insure a long-continued and honest administration of its powers. Were I called upon to decide, whether the people had best be omitted in the legislative or judiciary department, I would say it is better to leave them out of the legislative. The execution of the laws is more important than the making them.

* * *

I wish to preserve the line drawn by the federal constitution between the general and particular governments as it stands at present, and to take every prudent means of preventing either from stepping over it. Though the experiment has not yet had a long enough course to show us from which quarter encroachments are most to be feared, yet it is easy to foresee, from the nature of things, that the encroachments of the State governments will tend to an excess of liberty which will correct itself, (as in the late instance,) while those of the general government will tend to monarchy, which will fortify itself from day to day, instead of working its own cure, as all experience shows. I would rather be exposed to the inconveniences attending too much liberty, than those attending too small a degree of it. Then it is important to strengthen the State governments ; and as this cannot be done by any change in the federal constitution, (for the preservation of that is all we need contend for,) it must be

done by the States themselves, erecting such barriers at
the constitutional line as cannot be surmounted either
by themselves or by the general government. The
only barrier in their power is a wise government. A
weak one will lose ground in every contest. To obtain a wise and an able government, I consider the following changes as important. Render the legislature
a desirable station by lessening the number of representatives (say to 100) and lengthening somewhat their
term, and proportion them equally among the electors.
Adopt also a better mode of appointing senators.
Render the Executive a more desirable post to men of
abilities by making it more independent of the legislature. To wit, let him be chosen by other electors, for
a longer time, and ineligible forever after. Responsibility is a tremendous engine in a free government.
Let him feel the whole weight of it then, by taking
away the shelter of his executive council. Experience
both ways has already established the superiority of
this measure. Render the judiciary respectable by every possible means, to wit, firm tenure in office, competent salaries, and reduction of their numbers. Men
of high learning and abilities are few in every country ;
and by taking in those who are not so, the able part of
the body have their hands tied by the unable. This
branch of the government will have the weight of the
conflict on their hands, because they will be the last
appeal of reason. These are my general ideas of
amendments ; but, preserving the ends, I should be
flexible and conciliatory as to the means.

* * *

Our country is too large to have all its affairs directed by a single government. Public servants at such
a distance, and from under the eye of their constituents, must, from the circumstance of distance, be unable to administer and overlook all the details neces-

sary for the good government of the citizens, and the same circumstance, by rendering detection impossible to their constituents, will invite the public agents to corruption, plunder and waste. And I do verily believe, that if the principle were to prevail, of a common law being in force in the United States, (which principle possesses the General Government at once of all the powers of the State governments, and reduces us to a single consolidated government,) it would become the most corrupt government on the earth. You have seen the practises by which the public servants have been able to cover their conduct, or, where that could not be done, delusions by which they have varnished it for the eye of their constituents. What an augmentation of the field for jobbing, speculating, plundering, office-building and office-hunting would be produced by an assumption of all the State powers into the hands of the General Government. The true theory of our Constitution is surely the wisest and best, that the States are independent as to everything within themselves, and united as to everything respecting foreign nations. Let the General Government be reduced to foreign concerns only, and let our affairs be disentangled from those of all other nations, except as to commerce, which the merchants will manage the better, the more they are left free to manage for themselves, and our General Government may be reduced to a very simple organization, and a very unexpensive one.

* * *

I suspect that the doctrine, that small States alone are fitted to be republics, will be exploded by experience, with some other brilliant fallacies accredited by Montesquieu and other political writers. Perhaps it will be found, that to obtain a just republic (and it is to secure our just rights that we resort to government at all) it must be so extensive as that local egoisms may never reach its greater part ; that on every particular question, a majority may be found in its councils free from particular interests, and giving, therefore, an uniform prevalence to the principles of justice.   The smaller the societies, the more violent and more convulsive their schisms.   We have chanced to live in an age which will probably be distinguished in history, for its experiments in government on a larger scale than has yet taken place.   But we shall not live to see the result.   The grosser absurdities, such as hereditary magistracies, we shall see exploded in our day, long experience having already pronounced condemnation against them.   But what is to be the substitute ?   This our children or grand children will answer.   We may be satisfied with the certain knowledge that none can ever be tried, so stupid, so unrighteous, so oppressive, so destructive of every end for which honest men enter into government, as that which their forefathers had established, and their fathers alone venture to tumble headlong from the stations they have so long abused. It is unfortunate, that the efforts of mankind to recover the freedom of which they have been so long deprived, will be accompanied with violence, with errors, and even with crimes.   But while we weep over the means, we must pray for the end.

* * *

I do not think it for the interest of the general government itself, and still less of the Union at large, that the State governments should be so little respected as they have been.   However, I dare say that in time all these as well as their central government, like the planets revolving round their common sun, acting and acted upon according to their respective weights and distances, will produce that beautiful equilibrium on which our Constitution is founded, and which I believe it will exhibit to the world in a degree of perfection, unexampled but in the planetary system itself. The enlightened statesman, therefore, will endeavor to preserve the weight and influence of every part, as too much given to any member of it would destroy the general equilibrium.

* * *

You * have found on your return a higher style of political difference than you had left here. I fear this is inseparable from the different constitutions of the human mind, and that degree of freedom which permits unrestrained expression. Political dissension is doubtless a less evil than the lethargy of despotism, but still it is a great evil, and it would be as worthy the efforts of the patriot as of the philosopher, to exclude its influence, if possibly, from social life. The good are rare enough at best. There is no reason to subdivide them by artificial lines. But whether we shall ever be able so far to perfect the principles of society, as that political opinions shall, in its intercourse, be as inoffensive as those of philosophy, mechanics, or any other, may be well doubted.

* * *

Where a constitution, like ours, wears a mixed aspect of monarchy and republicanism, its citizens will naturally divide into two classes of sentiment, according as their tone of body or mind, their habits, connections and callings, induce them to wish to strengthen either the monarchial or the republican features of the Constitution. Some will consider it as an elective monarchy, which had better be made hereditary, and therefore endeavor to lead towards that all the forms and principles of its administration. Others will view it as an energetic republic, turning in all its points on

* Thomas Pinckney.

the pivot of free and frequent elections. The great body of our native citizens are unquestionably of the republican sentiment.

* * *

The whole body of the nation is the sovereign legislative, judiciary and executive power for itself. The inconvenience of meeting to exercise these powers in person, and their inaptitude to exercise them, induce them to appoint special organs to declare their legislative will, to judge and to execute it. It is the will of the nation which makes the law obligatory ; it is their will which creates or annihilates the organ which is to declare and announce it.

* * *

I tolerate with the utmost latitude the right of others to differ from me in opinion without imputing to them criminality. I know too well the weakness and uncertainty of human reason to wonder at its different results. Both of our political parties, at least the honest part of them, agree conscientiously in the same object — the public good ; but they differ essentially in what they deem the means of promoting that good. One side believes it best done by one composition of the governing powers ; the other, by a different one. One fears most the ignorance of the people ; the other, the selfishness of rulers independent of them. Which is right, time and experience will prove. We think that one side of this experiment has been long enough tried, and proved not to promote the good of the many ; and that the other has not been fairly and sufficiently tried. Our opponents think the reverse. With whichever opinion the body of the nation concurs, that must prevail. My anxieties on this subject will never carry me beyond the use of fair and honorable means, of truth and reason ; nor have they ever lessened my esteem for moral worth, nor alienated my affections from a single friend, who did not first withdraw himself.

* * *

What in fact is the difference of principle between the two parties here ? The one desires to preserve an entire independence of the executive and legislative branches on each other, and the dependence of both on the same source — the free election of the people. The other party wishes to lessen the dependence of the Executive and of one branch of the Legislature on the people, some by making them hold for life, some hereditary, and some even for giving the Executive an influence by patronage or corruption over the remaining popular branch, so as to reduce the elective franchise to its minimum.

* * *

As the division into whig and tory is founded in the nature of man ; the weakly and nerveless, the rich and the corrupt, seeing more safety and accessibility in a strong executive ; the healthy, firm, and virtuous, feeling a confidence in their physical and moral resources, and willing to part with only so much power as is necessary for their good government ; and, therefore, to retain the rest in the hands of the many, the division will substantially be into whig and tory, as in England formerly.

* * *

But the true barriers of our liberty in this country are our State governments ; and the wisest conservative power ever contrived by man, is that of which our Revolution and present government found us possessed. Seventeen distinct States, amalgamated into one as to their foreign concerns, but single and independent as to their internal administration, regularly organized with a legislature and governor resting on the choice of the people, and enlightened by a free press, can never be so fascinated by the arts of one man, as to submit voluntarily to his usurpation. Nor can they be constrained to it by any force he can possess. While that may paralyze the single State in which it happens to be encamped, sixteen others, spread over a country of two thousand miles diameter, rise up on every side, ready organized for deliberation by a constitutional legislature, and for action by their governor, constitutionally the commander of the militia of the State, that is to say, of every man in it able to bear arms ; and that militia, too, regularly formed into regiments and battalions, into infantry, cavalry and artillery, trained under officers general and subordinate, legally appointed, always in readiness, and to whom they are already in habits of obedience.

* * *

I do not know whether I am able at present to form a just idea of the situation of our country. If I am, it is such as, during the *bellum omnium in omnia* of Europe, will require the union of all its friends to resist its enemies within and without. If we schismatize on either men or measures, if we do not act in phalanx, as when we rescued it from the satellites of monarchism, I will not say our *party*, the term is false and degrading, but our *nation* will be undone. For the republicans are the *nation*. Their opponents are but a faction, weak in numbers, but powerful and profuse in the command of money, and backed by a nation, powerful also and profuse in the use of the same means ; and the more profuse, in both cases, as the money they thus employ is not their own but their creditors, to be paid off by a bankruptcy, which whether it pays a dollar or a shilling in the pound is of little concern with them. The last hope of human liberty in this world rests on us. We ought, for so dear a state, to sacrifice every attachment and every enmity. Leave the President free to choose his own coadjutors, to pursue his own measures, and support him and them, even if we think we are wiser than they, honester than they are, or possessing more enlarged information of the state of things. If we move in mass, be it ever so circuitously, we shall attain our object; but if we break into squads, every one pursuing the path he thinks most direct, we become an easy conquest to those who can now barely hold us in check. I repeat again, that we ought not to schismatize on either men or measures. Principles alone can justify that. If we find our government in all its branches rushing headlong, like our predecessors, into the arms of monarchy, if we find them violating our dearest rights, the trial by jury, the freedom of the press, the freedom of opinion, civil or religious, or opening on our peace of mind or personal safety the sluices of terrorism, if we see them raising standing armies, when the absence of all other danger points to these as the sole objects on which they are to be employed, then indeed let us withdraw and call the nation to its tents. But while our functionaries are wise, and honest, and vigilant, let us move compactly under their guidance, and we have nothing to fear. Things may here and there go a little wrong. It is not in their power to prevent it. But all will be right in the end, though not perhaps by the shortest means.

You * know, my dear Sir, that this union of republicans has been the constant theme of my exhortations, that I have ever refused to know any subdivisions among them, to take part in any personal differences; and therefore you will not give to the present observations any other than general application. I may sometimes differ in opinion from some of

* Colonel William Duane.

my friends, from those whose views are as pure and sound as my own. I censure none, but do homage to every one's right of opinion.

* * *

Possessing ourselves the combined blessing of liberty and order, we wish the same to other countries, and to none more than yours,* which, the first of civilized nations, presented examples of what man should be. Not, indeed, that the forms of government adapted to their age and country are practicable or to be imitated in our day, although prejudices in their favor would be natural enough to your people. The circumstances of the world are too much changed for that. The equal rights of man, and the happiness of every individual, are now acknowledged to be the only legitimate objects of government. Modern times have the signal advantage, too, of having discovered the only device by which these rights can be secured, to-wit : government by the people, acting not in person, but by representatives chosen by themselves, that is to say, by every man of ripe years and sane mind, who either contributes by his purse or person to the support of his country.

* * *

At the birth of our republic, I committed that opinion to the world, in the draught of a constitution annexed to the "Notes on Virginia," in which a provision was inserted for a representation permanently equal. The infancy of the subject at that moment, and our inexperience of self-government, occasioned gross departures in that draught from genuine republican canons. In truth, the abuses of monarchy had so much filled all the space of political contemplation, that we imagined everything republican which was not monarchy. We had not yet penetrated to the mother

* France. Written to M. Coray.

principle, that "governments are republican only in proportion as they embody the will of their people, and execute it." Hence, our first constitutions had really no leading principles in them. But experience and reflection have but more and more confirmed me in the particular importance of the equal representation then proposed. Where then is our republicanism to be found? Not in our constitution certainly, but merely in the spirit of our people. That would oblige even a despot to govern us republicanly. Owing to this spirit, and to nothing in the form of our constitution, all things have gone well.

Only lay down true principles, and adhere to them inflexibly. Do not be frightened into their surrender by the alarms of the timid, or the croakings of wealth against the ascendency of the people. If experience be called for, appeal to that of our fifteen or twenty governments for forty years, and show me where the people have done half the mischief in these forty years, that a single despot would have done in a single year; or show half the riots and rebellions, the crimes and the punishments, which have taken place in any single nation, under kingly government, during the same period. The true foundation of republican government is the equal right of every citizen, in his person and property, and in their management. Try by this, as a tally, every provision of our constitution, and see if it hangs directly on the will of the people. Reduce your legislature to a convenient number for full, but orderly discussion. Let every man who fights or pays, exercise his just and equal right in their election. Submit them to approbation or rejection at short intervals. Let the executive be chosen in the same way, and for the same term, by those whose agent he is to be; and leave no screen of a council behind which to skulk from responsibility.

The organization of our county administrations may

be thought more difficult. But follow principle, and
the knot unties itself. Divide the counties into wards
of such size as that every citizen can attend, when
called on, and act in person. Ascribe to them the
government of their wards in all things relating to
themselves exclusively. A justice, chosen by themselves, in each, a constable, a military company, a pa-
trol, a school, the care of their own poor, their own
portion of the public roads, the choice of one or more
jurors to serve in some court, and the delivery, within
their own wards, of their own votes for all elective officers of higher sphere, will relieve the county administration of nearly all its business, will have it better
done, and by making every citizen an acting member
of the government, and in the offices nearest and most
interesting to him, will attach him by his strongest feelings to the independence of his country, and its republican constitution. The justices thus chosen by
every ward, would constitute the county court, would
do its judiciary business, direct roads and bridges, levy
county and poor rates, and administer all the matters
of common interest to the whole country. These
wards, called townships in New England, are the vital
principle of their governments, and have proved themselves the wisest invention ever devised by the wit of
man for the perfect exercise of self-government, and
for its preservation. We should thus marshal our government into, 1, the general federal republic, for all
concerns foreign and federal ; 2, that of the State, for
what relates to our own citizens exclusively ; 3, the
county republics, for the duties and concerns of the
county ; and 4, the ward republics, for the small, and
yet numerous and interesting concerns of the neighborhood ; and in government, as well as in every other
business of life, it is by division and subdivision of duties alone, that all matters, great and small, can be managed to perfection. And the whole is cemented by

giving to every citizen, personally, a part in the administration of the public affairs.

The sum of these amendments is, 1. General suffrage. 2. Equal representation in the legislature. 3. An executive chosen by the people. 4. Judges elective or amovable. 5. Justices, jurors, and sheriffs elective. 6. Ward divisions. And 7. Periodical amendments of the constitution.

Private fortunes are destroyed by public as well as by private extravagance. And this is the tendency of all human governments. A departure from principle in one instance becomes a precedent for a second ; that second for a third ; and so on, till the bulk of the society is reduced to be mere automatons of misery, to have no sensibilities left but for sinning and suffering. Then begins, indeed, the *bellum omnium in omnia*, which some philosophers observing to be so general in this world, have mistaken it for the natural, instead of the abusive state of man. And the fore horse of this frightful team in public debt. Taxation follows that, and in its train wretchedness and oppression.

* * *

It is a fatal heresy to suppose that either our State governments are superior to the federal, or the federal to the States. The people, to whom all authority belongs, have divided the powers of government into two distinct departments, the leading characters of which are *foreign* and domestic ; and they have appointed for each a distinct set of functionaries. These they have made co-ordinate, checking and balancing each other, like the three cardinal departments in the individual States : each equally supreme as to the powers delegated to itself, and neither authorized ultimately to decide what belongs to itself, or to its coparcenor in government. As independent, in fact, as different nations, a spirit of forbearance and compromise, therefore, and not of encroachment and usurpation, is the healing balm of such a constitution; and each party should prudently shrink from all approach to the line of demarcation, instead of rashly overleaping it, or throwing grapples ahead to haul to hereafter. But, finally, the peculiar happiness of our blessed system is, that in differences of opinion between these different sets of servants, the appeal is to neither, but to their employers peaceably assembled by their representatives in Convention. This is more rational than the *jus fortioris*, or the cannon's mouth, the *ultima et sola ratio regum.*

* * *

In answer to your * inquiry as to the merits of Gillies' translation of the Politics of Aristotle, I can only say that it has the reputation of being preferable to Ellis', the only rival translation into English. I have never seen it myself, and therefore do not speak of it from my own knowledge. But so different was the style of society then, and with those people, from what it is now and with us, that I think little edification can be obtained from their writings on the subject of government. They had just ideas of the value of personal liberty, but none at all of the structure of government best calculated to preserve it. They knew no medium between a democracy (the only pure republic, but impracticable beyond the limits of a town) and an abandonment of themselves to an aristocracy, or a tyranny independent of the people. It seems not to have occurred that where the citizens cannot meet to transact their business in person, they alone have the right to choose the agents who shall transact it; and that in this way a republican, or popular government, of the second grade of purity, may be exercised over any extent of country. The full experiment of a government

* Isaac H. Tiffany.

democratical, but representative, was and is still reserved for us. The idea (taken, indeed, from the little specimen formerly existing in the English constitution, but now lost) has been carried by us, more or less, into all our legislative and executive departments ; but it has not yet, by any of us, been pushed into all the ramifications of the system, so far as to leave no authority existing not responsible to the people ; whose rights, however, to the exercise and fruits of their own industry, can never be protected against the selfishness of rulers not subject to their control at short periods. The introduction of this new principle of representative democracy has rendered useless almost everything written before on the structure of government ; and, in a great measure, relieves our regret, if the political writings of Aristotle, or of any other ancient, have been lost, or are unfaithfully rendered or explained to us. My most earnest wish is to see the republican element of popular control pushed to the maximum of its practicable exercise. I shall then believe that our government may be pure and perpetual.

* * *

The first principle of republicanism is, that the *lex-majoris partis* is the fundamental law of every society of individuals of equal rights ; to consider the will of the society enounced by the majority of a single vote, as sacred as if unanimous, is the first of all lessons in importance, yet the last which is thoroughly learnt. This law once disregarded, no other remains but that of force, which ends necessarily in military despotism.

* * *

At the first session of our legislature after the Declaration of Independence, we passed a law abolishing entails. And this was followed by one abolishing the privilege of primogeniture, and dividing the lands of intestates equally among all their children, or other representatives. These laws, drawn by myself, laid the axe to the foot of pseudo-aristocracy. And had another which I prepared been adopted by the legislature, our work would have been complete. It was a bill for the more general diffusion of learning. This proposed to divide every county into wards of five or six miles square, like your townships; to establish in each ward a free school for reading, writing and common arithmetic; to provide for the annual selection of the best subjects from these schools, who might receive, at the public expense, a higher degree of education at a district school; and from these district schools to select a certain number of the most promising subjects, to be completed at an University, where all the useful sciences should be taught. Worth and genius would thus have been sought out from every condition of life, and completely prepared by education for defeating the competition of wealth and birth for public trusts. The law for religious freedom, which made a part of this system, having put down the aristocracy of the clergy, and restored to the citizen the freedom of the mind, and those of entails and descents nurturing an equality of condition among them, this on education would have raised the mass of the people to the high ground of moral respectability necessary to their own safety, and to orderly government; and would have completed the great object of qualifying them to select the veritable aristoi, for the trusts of government, to the exclusion of the pseudalists. Although this law has not yet been acted on but in a small and inefficient degree, it is still considered as before the legislature, with other bills of the revised code, not yet taken up, and I have great hope that some patriotic spirit will, at a favorable moment, call it up, and make it the key-stone of the arch of our government.

For I agree with you * that there is a natural aristocracy among men. The grounds of this are virtue and talents. Formerly, bodily powers gave place among the aristoi. But since the invention of gunpowder has armed the weak as well as the strong with missile death, bodily strength, like beauty, good humor, politeness and other accomplishments, has become but an auxiliary ground of distinction. There is also an artificial aristocracy, founded on wealth and birth, without either virtue or talents; for with these it would belong to the first class. The natural aristocracy I consider as the most precious gift of nature, for the instruction, the trusts, and government of society. And indeed, it would have been inconsistent in creation to have formed man for the social state, and not to have provided virtue and wisdom enough to manage the concerns of the society. May we not even say, that that form of government is the best, which provides the most effectually for a pure selection of these natural aristoi into the offices of government ? The artificial aristocracy is a mischievous ingredient in government, and provision should be made to prevent its ascendency. On the question, what is the best provision, you and I differ ; but we differ as rational friends, using the free exercise of our own reason, and mutually indulging its errors. You think it best to put the pseudo-aristoi into a separate chamber of legislation, where they may be hindered from doing mischief by their co-ordinate branches, and where, also, they may be a protection to wealth against the Agrarian and plundering enterprises of the majority of the people. I think that to give them power in order to prevent them from doing mischief, is arming them for it, and increasing instead of remedying the evil. For if the co-ordinate branches can arrest their action, so may they that of the co-ordinates. Mischief may be done negatively as well as positively. Of this, a cabal in the Senate of the

* John Adams.

United States has furnished many proofs. Nor do I believe them necessary to protect the wealthy ; because enough of these will find their way into every branch of the legislation, to protect themselves. From fifteen to twenty legislatures of our own, in action for thirty years past, have proved that no fears of an equalization of property are to be apprehended from them. I think the best remedy is exactly that provided by all our constitutions, to leave to the citizens the free election and separation of the aristoi from the pseudo-aristoi, of the wheat from the chaff. In general they will elect the really good and wise. In some instances, wealth may corrupt, and birth blind them ; but not in sufficient degree to endanger the society. It is probable that our difference of opinion may, in some measure, be produced by a difference of character in those among whom we live.

With respect to aristocracy, we should further consider, that before the establishment of the American States, nothing was known to history but the man of the old world, crowded within limits either small or overcharged, and steeped in the vices which that situation generates. A government adapted to such men would be one thing ; but a very different one, that for the man of these States. Here every one may have land to labor for himself, if he chooses ; or, preferring the exercise of any other industry, may exact for it such compensation as not only to afford a comfortable subsistence, but wherewith to provide for a cessation from labor in old age. Every one, by his property, or by his satisfactory situation, is interested in the support of law and order. And such men may safely and advantageously reserve to themselves a wholesome control over their public affairs, and a degree of freedom, which, in the hands of the *canaille* of the cities of Europe, would be instantly perverted to the demolition and destruction of everything public and private. The history of the last twenty-five years of France, and of the last forty years in America, nay of its last two hundred years, proves the truth of both parts of this observation.

*   *   *

The question you * propose, whether circumstances do not sometimes occur, which make it a duty in officers of high trust, to assume authorities beyond the law, is easy of solution in principle, but sometimes embarrassing in practice. A strict observance of the written laws is doubtless *one* of the high duties of a good citizen, but it is not *the highest*. The laws of necessity, of self-preservation, of saving our country when in danger, are of higher obligation. To lose our country by a scrupulous adherence to written law, would be to lose the law itself, with life, liberty, property and all those who are enjoying them with us ; thus absurdly sacrificing the end to the means. When, in the battle of Germantown, General Washington's army was annoyed from Chew's house, he did not hesitate to plant his cannon against it, although the property of a citizen. When he besieged Yorktown, he leveled the suburbs, feeling that the laws of property must be postponed to the safety of the nation. While the army was before York, the Governor of Virginia took horses, carriages, provisions and even men by force, to enable that army to stay together till it could master the public enemy ; and he was justified. A ship at sea in distress for provisions, meets another having abundance, yet refusing a supply ; the law of self-preservation authorizes the distressed to take a supply by force. In all these cases, the unwritten laws of necessity, of self-preservation, and of the public safety, control the written laws of *meum* and *tuum*.

*   *   *

* J. B. Colvin.

Under the maxim of the law itself, that *inter arma silent leges,* that in an encampment expecting daily attack from a powerful enemy, self-preservation is paramount to all law, I expected that instead of invoking the forms of the law to cover traitors, all good citizens would have concurred in securing them. Should we have ever gained our Revolution, if we had bound our hands by manacles of the law, not only in the beginning, but in any part of the revolutionary conflict? There are extreme cases where the laws become inadequate even to their own preservation, and where the universal resource is a dictator, or martial law.

* * *

* The most interesting intelligence from America, is that respecting the late insurrection in Massachusetts. I am not discouraged by this. For thus I calculate. An insurrection in one of thirteen States, in the course of eleven years that they have subsisted, amounts to one in any particular State, in one hundred and forty-three years, say a century and a half. This would not be near as many, as have happened in every other government that has ever existed. So that we shall have the difference between a light and a heavy government, as clear gain. I have no fear, but that the result of our experiment will be, that men may be trusted to govern themselves without a master. Could the contrary of this be proved, I should conclude, either that there is no God, or that he is a malevolent being.

* * *

The British ministry have so long hired their gazetteers to repeat, and model into every form, lies about our being in anarchy, that the world has at length believed them, the English nation has believed them, the ministers themselves have come to believe them, and

* Written from Paris, July 2, 1787.

what is more wonderful, we have believed them ourselves. Yet where does this anarchy exist ? Where
did it ever exist, except in the single instance of Massachusetts ? And can history produce an instance of
rebellion so honorably conducted ? I say nothing of
its motives. They were founded in ignorance, not
wickedness. God forbid we should ever be twenty
years without such a rebellion. The people cannot be
all, and always, well informed. The part which is
wrong will be discontented, in proportion to the importance of the facts they misconceive. If they remain quiet under such misconceptions, it is a lethargy,
the forerunner of death to the public liberty. We
have had thirteen States independent for eleven years.
There has been one rebellion. That comes to one rebellion in a century and a half, for each State. What
country before, ever existed a century and a half without a rebellion ? And what country can preserve its liberties, if its rulers are not warned from time to time, that
this people preserve the spirit of resistance ? Let them
take arms. The remedy is to set them right as to facts,
pardon and pacify them. What signify a few lives
lost in a century or two ? The tree of liberty must be
refreshed from time to time, with the blood of patriots
and tyrants. It is its natural manure. Our convention
has been too much impressed by the insurrection of
Massachusetts ; and on the spur of the moment, they
are setting up a kite to keep the hen yard in order.

* * *

It has been said, too, that our governments, both federal and particular, want energy ; that it is difficult to
restrain both individuals and States from committing
wrong. This is true, and it is an inconvenience. On
the other hand, that energy which absolute governments derive from an armed force, which is the effect
of the bayonet constantly held at the breast of every

citizen, and which resembles very much the stillness of the grave, must be admitted also to have its inconveniences. We weigh the two together, and like best to submit to the former. Compare the number of wrongs committed with impunity by citizens among us with those committed by the sovereign in other countries, and the last will be found most numerous, most oppressive on the mind, and most degrading of the dignity of man.

ECONOMIC PHILOSOPHY

In the earlier times of the colony, when lands were to be obtained for little or nothing, some provident individuals procured large grants ; and, desirous of founding great families for themselves, settled them on their descendants in fee tail. The transmission of this property from generation to generation, in the same name, raised up a distinct set of families, who, being privileged by law in the perpetuation of their wealth, were thus formed into a Patrician order, distinguished by the splendor and luxury of their establishments. From this order, too, the king habitually selected his counsellors of State ; the hope of which distinction devoted the whole corps to the interests and will of the crown. To annul this privilege, and instead of an aristocracy of wealth, of more harm and danger, than benefit, to society, to make an opening for the aristocracy of virtue and talent, which nature has wisely provided for the direction of the interests of society, and scattered with equal hand through all its conditions, was deemed essential to a well-ordered republic. — To effect it, no violence was necessary, no deprivation of natural right, but rather an enlargement of it by a repeal of the law. For this would authorize the present holder to divide the property among his children equally, as his affections were divided ; and

would place them, by natural generation, on the level
of their fellow citizens.   *first born*

I proposed to abolish the law of primogeniture, and
to make real estate descendible in parcenary to the next
of kin, as personal property is, by the statute of distribution.   Mr. Pendleton * wished to preserve the right
of primogeniture, but seeing at once that that could
not prevail, he proposed we should adopt the Hebrew
principle, and give a double portion to the elder son.
I observed, that if the eldest son could eat twice as
much, or do double work, it might be a natural evidence of his right to a double portion ; but being on a
par in his powers and wants, with his brothers and
sisters, he should be on a par also in the partition of the
patrimony ; and such was the decision of the other
members.

*   *   *

If Legislative services are worth mentioning, and the
stamp of liberality and equality, which was necessary
to be imposed on our laws in the first crisis of our birth
as a nation, was of any value, they will find that the
leading and most important laws of that day were prepared by myself, and carried chiefly by my efforts ;
supported, indeed, by able and faithful coadjutors from
the ranks of the House, very effective as seconds, but
who would not have taken the field as leaders.

The prohibition of the further importation of slaves
was the first of these measures in time.

This was followed by the abolition of entails, which
broke up the hereditary and high-handed aristocracy,
which, by accumulating immense masses of property
in single lines of families, had divided our country into
two distinct orders, of nobles and plebeians.

But further to complete the equality among our citizens so essential to the maintenance of republican government, it was necessary to abolish the principle of

* Edmund Pendleton.

primogeniture. I drew the law of descents, giving equal inheritance to sons and daughters, which made a part of the revised code.

* * *

The greatest evils of populous society have ever appeared to me to spring from the vicious distribution of its members among the occupations called for. I have no doubt that those nations are essentially right, which leaves this to individual choice, as a better guide to an advantageous distribution than any other which could be devised. But when, by a blind concourse, particular occupations are ruinously overcharged, and others left in want of hands, the national authorities can do much towards restoring the equilibrium. On the revival of letters, learning became the universal favorite. And with reason, because there was not enough of it existing to manage the affairs of a nation to the best advantage, nor to advance its individuals to the happiness of which they were susceptible, by improvements in their minds, their morals, their health, and in those conveniences which contribute to the comfort and embellishment of life. All the efforts of the society, therefore, were directed to the increase of learning, and the inducements of respect, ease, and profit were held up for its encouragement. Even the charities of the nation forgot that misery was their object, and spent themselves in founding schools to transfer to science the hardy sons of the plough. To these incitements were added the powerful fascinations of great cities. These circumstances have long since produced an overcharge in the class of competitors for learned occupation, and great distress among the supernumerary candidates ; and the more, as their habits of life have disqualified them for re-entering into the laborious class. The evil cannot be suddenly, nor perhaps ever entirely cured : nor should I presume to say by what means it may be cured. Doubtless there are many engines which the nation might bring to bear on this object. Public opinion, and public encouragement are among these. The class principally defective is that of agriculture. It is the first in utility, and ought to be the first in respect. The same artificial means which have been used to produce a competition in learning, may be equally successful in restoring agriculture to its primary dignity in the eyes of men. It is a science of the very first order. It counts among its handmaids the most respectable sciences, such as Chemistry, Natural Philosophy, Mechanics, Mathematics generally, Natural History, Botany. In every College and University, a professorship of agriculture, and the class of its students, might be honored as the first. Young men closing their academical education with this, as the crown of all other sciences, fascinated with its solid charms, and at a time when they are to choose an occupation, instead of crowding the other classes, would return to the farms of their fathers, their own, or those of others, and replenish and invigorate a calling, now languishing under contempt and oppression. The charitable schools, instead of storing their pupils with a lore which the present state of society does not call for, converted into schools of agriculture, might restore them to that branch qualified to enrich and honor themselves, and to increase the productions of the nation instead of consuming them.

＊　＊　＊

We have now lands enough to employ an infinite number of people in their cultivation. Cultivators of the earth are the most valuable citizens. They are the most vigorous, the most independent, the most virtuous, and they are tied to their country, and wedded to its liberty and interests, by the most lasting bonds. As long, therefore, as they can find employment in this line, I would not convert them into mariners, artisans, or anything else. But our citizens will find employment in this line, till their numbers, and of course their productions, become too great for the demand, both internal and foreign. This is not the case as yet, and probably will not be for a considerable time. As soon as it is, the surplus of hands must be turned to something else. I should then, perhaps, wish to turn them to the sea in preference to manufactures ; because, comparing the characters of the two classes, I find the former the most valuable citizens. I consider the class of artificers as the panders of vice, and the instruments by which the liberties of a country are generally overturned. However, we are not free to decide this question on principles of theory only. Our people are decided in the opinion, that it is necessary for us to take a share in the occupation of the ocean, and their established habits induce them to require that the sea be kept open to them, and that that line of policy be pursued, which will render the use of that element to them as great as possible. I think it a duty in those entrusted with the administration of their affairs, to conform themselves to the decided choice of their constituents ; and that therefore, we should, in every instance, preserve an equality of right to them in the transportation of commodities, in the right of fishing, and in the other uses of the sea.

* * *

You * ask what I think on the expediency of encouraging our States to be commercial ? Were I to indulge my own theory, I should wish them to practise neither commerce nor navigation, but to stand, with respect to Europe, precisely on the footing of China. We should thus avoid wars, and all our citizens would be husbandmen. Whenever, indeed, our numbers should so increase as that our produce would overstock the markets of those nations who should come to seek it, the farmers must either employ the surplus of their time in manu-

* Mr. Hogendorp.

factures, or the surplus of our hands must be employed in manufactures or in navigation. But that day would, I think, be distant, and we should long keep our workmen in Europe, while Europe should be drawing rough materials, and even subsistence from America. But this is theory only, and a theory which the servants of America are not at liberty to follow. Our people have a decided taste for navigation and commerce. They take this from their mother country ; and their servants are in duty bound to calculate all their measures on this datum : we wish to do it by throwing open all the doors of commerce, and knocking off its shackles. But as this cannot be done for others, unless they will do it for us, and there is no great probability that Europe will do this, I suppose we shall be obliged to adopt a system which may shackle them in our ports, as they do us in theirs.

* * *

No war can be safe for us which threatens France with an unfavorable issue ; and in the next, it will probably embark us again into the ocean of speculation, engage us to over-trade ourselves, convert us into searovers, under French and Dutch colors, divert us from agriculture, which is our wisest pursuit, because it will in the end contribute most to real wealth, good morals, and happiness. The wealth acquired by speculation and plunder, is fugacious in its nature, and fills society with the spirit of gambling. The moderate and sure income of husbandry begets permanent improvement, quiet life, and orderly conduct, both public and private. We have no occasion for more commerce than to take off our superfluous produce.

* * *

For though I am decidedly of opinion we should take no part in European quarrels, but cultivate peace and commerce with all, yet who can avoid seeing the source *surplus will exceed Europe*

of war, in the tyranny of those nations, who deprive us of the natural right of trading with our neighbors? The produce of the United States will soon exceed the European demand; what is to be done with the surplus, when there shall be one? It will be employed, without question, to open, by force, a market for itself, with those placed on the same continent with us, and who wish nothing better.

* * *

Is commerce so much the basis of the existence of the United States as to call for a bankrupt law? On the contrary, are we not almost merely agricultural? Should not all laws be made with a view essentially to the poor husbandmen? When laws are wanting for particular descriptions of other callings, should not the husbandmen be carefully excused from their operation, and preserved under that of the general system only; which general system is fitted to the condition of husbandmen?

* * *

The differences of circumstance between this and the old countries of Europe, furnish differences of fact whereon to reason, in questions of political economy, and will consequently produce sometimes a difference of result. There, for instance, the quantity of food is fixed, or increasing in a slow and only arithmetical ratio, and the proportion is limited by the same ratio. Supernumerary births consequently add only to your * mortality. Here the immense extent of uncultivated and fertile lands enables every one who will labor to marry young, and to raise a family of any size. Our food, then, may increase geometrically with our laborers, and our births, however multiplied, become effective. Again, there the best distribution of labor is supposed to be that which places the manufacturing hands along-

* Written to M. Jean Baptiste Say.

side the agricultural ; so that the one part shall feed both, and the other part furnish both with clothes and other comforts. Would that be best here ? Egoism and first appearances say yes. Or would it be better that all our laborers should be employed in agriculture ? In this case a double or treble portion of fertile lands would be brought into culture ; a double or treble creation of food be produced, and its surplus go to nourish the now perishing births of Europe, who in return would manufacture and send us in exchange our clothes and other comforts. Morality listens to this, and so invariably do the laws of nature create our duties and interests, that when they seem to be at variance, we ought to suspect some fallacy in our reasonings. In solving this question, too, we should allow its just weight to the moral and physical preference of the agricultural, over the manufacturing, man.

* * *

The political economists of Europe have established it as a principle, that every State should endeavor to manufacture for itself ; and this principle, like many others, we transfer to America, without calculating the difference of circumstance which should often produce a difference of result. In Europe the lands are either cultivated, or locked up against the cultivator. Manufacture must therefore be resorted to of necessity not of choice, to support the surplus of their people. But we have an immensity of land courting the industry of the husbandman. Is it best then that all our citizens should be employed in its improvement, or that one half should be called off from that to exercise manufactures and handicraft arts for the other ? Those who labor in the earth are the chosen people of God, if ever He had a chosen people, whose breasts He has made His peculiar deposit for substantial and genuine virtue. It is the focus in which he keeps alive that sacred fire, which otherwise might escape from the face of the earth. Corruption of morals in the mass of cultivators is a phenomenon of which no age nor nation has furnished an example. It is the mark set on those, who, not looking up to heaven, to their own soil and industry, as does the husbandman, for their subsistence, depend for it on casualties and caprice of customers. Dependence begets subservience and venality, suffocates the germ of virtue, and prepares fit tools for the designs of ambition. This, the natural progress and consequence of the arts, has sometimes perhaps been retarded by accidental circumstances ; but, generally speaking, the proportion which the aggregate of the other classes of citizens bears in any State to that of its husbandmen, is the proportion of its unsound to its healthy parts, and is a good enough barometer whereby to measure its degree of corruption. While we have land to labor then, let us never wish to see our citizens occupied at a workbench, or twirling a distaff. Carpenters, masons, smiths, are wanting in husbandry ; but, for the general operations of manufacture, let our workshops remain in Europe. It is better to carry provisions and materials to workmen there, than bring them to the provisions and materials, and with them their manners and principles. The loss by the transportation of commodities across the Atlantic will be made up in happiness and permanence of government. The mobs of great cities add just so much to the support of pure government, as sores do to the strength of the human body. It is the manners and spirit of a people which preserve a republic in vigor. A degeneracy in these is a canker which soon eats to the heart of its laws and constitution.

* * *

You * tell me I am quoted by those who wish to continue our dependence on England for manufactures.

* Benjamin Austin.

There was a time when I might have been so quoted
with more candor, but within the thirty years which
have since elapsed, how are circumstances changed !
We were then in peace. Our independent place among
nations was acknowledged. A commerce which offered
the raw material in exchange for the same material after
receiving the last touch of industry, was worthy of
welcome to all nations. It was expected that those
especially to whom manufacturing industry was important, would cherish the friendship of such customers
by every favor, by every inducement, and particularly
cultivate their peace by every act of justice and friendship. Under this prospect the question seemed legitimate, whether, with such an immensity of unimproved
land, courting the hand of husbandry, the industry of
agriculture, or that of manufactures, would add most to
the national wealth ? And the doubt was entertained
on this consideration chiefly, that to the labor of the
husbandman a vast addition is made by the spontaneous
energies of the earth on which it is employed : for one
grain of wheat committed to the earth, she renders
twenty, thirty, and even fifty fold, whereas to the labor
of the manufacturer nothing is added. Pounds of flax,
in his hands, yield, on the contrary, but pennyweights
of lace. This exchange, too, laborious as it might seem,
what a field did it promise for the occupations of the
ocean ; what a nursery for that class of citizens who
were to exercise and maintain our equal rights on that
element ? This was the state of things in 1785, when
the "Notes on Virginia" were first printed ; when, the
ocean being open to all nations, and their common right
in it acknowledged and exercised under regulations
sanctioned by the assent and usage of all, it was thought
that the doubt might claim some consideration. But
who in 1785 could foresee the rapid depravity which
was to render the close of that century the disgrace of
the history of man ?

We must now place the manufacturer by the side of the agriculturist. The former question is suppressed, or rather assumes a new form. Shall we make our own comforts, or go without them, at the will of a foreign nation ? He, therefore, who is now against domestic manufacture, must be for reducing us either to dependence on that foreign nation, or to be clothed in skins, and to live like wild beasts in dens and caverns. I am not one of these ; experience has taught me that manufactures are now as necessary to our independence as to our comfort ; and if those who quote me as of a different opinion, will keep pace with me in purchasing nothing foreign where an equivalent of domestic fabric can be obtained, without regard to difference of price, it will not be our fault if we do not soon have a supply at home equal to our demand, and wrest that weapon of distress from the hand which has wielded it. If it shall be proposed to go beyond our own supply, the question of '85 will then recur, will our *surplus* labor be then most beneficially employed in the culture of the earth, or in the fabrications of art ? We have time yet for consideration, before that question will press upon us ; and the maxim to be applied will depend on the circumstances which shall then exist ; for in so complicated a science as political economy, no one axiom can be laid down as wise and expedient for all times and circumstances, and for their contraries.

* * *

I had under my eye, when writing, the manufacturers of the great cities in the old countries, at the time present, with whom the want of food and clothing necessary to sustain life, has begotten a depravity of morals, a dependence and corruption, which renders them an undesirable accession to a country whose morals are sound. My expressions looked forward to the time when our own great cities would get into the same state. But they have been quoted as if meant for the present time here. As yet our manufacturers are as much at their ease, as independent and moral as our agricultural inhabitants, and they will continue so as long as there are vacant lands for them to resort to ; because whenever it shall be attempted by the other classes to reduce them to the minimum of subsistence, they will quit their trades and go to laboring the earth. A first question is, whether it is desirable for us to receive at present the dissolute and demoralized handicraftsmen of the old cities of Europe ? A second and more difficult one is, when even good handicraftsmen arrive here, is it better for them to set up their trade, or go to the culture of the earth ? Whether their labor in their trade is worth more than their labor on the soil, increased by the creative energies of the earth ?

Amidst the pressure of evils with which the belligerent edicts have afflicted us, some permanent good will arise ; the spring given to manufacturers will have durable effects. Knowing most of my own State, I can affirm with confidence that were free intercourse opened again to-morrow, she would never again import one-half of the coarse goods which she has done down to the date of the edicts. These will be made in our families. For finer goods we must resort to the larger manufactories established in the towns. Some jealousy of this spirit of manufacture seems excited among commercial men. It would have been as just when we first began to make our own ploughs and hoes. They have certainly lost the profit of bringing these from a foreign country. My idea is that we should encourage home manufactures to the extent of our own consumption of everything of which we raise the raw material. I do not think it fair in the ship-owners to say we ought not to make our own axes, nails, &c., here, that they may have the benefit of carrying the iron to Europe, and bringing back the axes, nails, &c. Our agriculture will still afford surplus produce enough to employ a due proportion of navigation.

* * *

I have lately inculcated the encouragement of manufactures to the extent of our own consumption at least, in all articles of which we raise the raw material. On this the federal papers and meetings have sounded the alarm of Chinese policy, destruction of commerce, &c. ; that is to say, the iron which we make must not be wrought here into ploughs, axes, hoes, &c., in order that the ship owner may have the profit of carrying it to Europe, and bringing it back in a manufactured form, as if after manufacturing our own raw materials for own use, there would not be a surplus produce sufficient to employ a due proportion of navigation in carrying it to market and exchanging it for those articles of which we have not the raw material. Yet this absurd hue and cry has contributed much to federalize New England, their doctrine goes to the sacrificing agriculture and manufactures to commerce ; to the calling all our people from the interior country to the sea-shore to turn merchants, and to convert this great agricultural country into a city of Amsterdam. But I trust the good sense of our country will see that its greatest prosperity depends on a due balance between agriculture, manufactures and commerce, and not in this protuberant navigation which has kept us in hot water from the commencement of our government, and is now engaging us in war.

* * *

An equilibrium of agriculture, manufactures, and commerce, is certainly become essential to our independence. Manufactures, sufficient for our own consumption, of what we raise the raw material, (and no more.) Commerce sufficient to carry the surplus produce of agriculture, beyond our own consumption, to a market for exchanging it for articles we cannot raise, (and no more.) These are the true limits of manufactures and commerce. To go beyond them is to increase our dependence on foreign nations, and our liability to war.

* * *

Indeed it seems to me that in proportion as commercial avarice and corruption advance on us from the north and east, the principles of free government are to retire to the agricultural states of the south and west, as their last asylum and bulwark.

MORALS AND RELIGION

Give up money, give up fame, give up science, give the earth itself and all it contains, rather than do an immoral act. And never suppose, that in any possible situation, or under any circumstances, it is best for you * to do a dishonorable thing, however slightly so it may appear to you. Whenever you are to do a thing, though it can never be known but to yourself, ask yourself how you would act were all the world looking at you, and act accordingly. Encourage all your virtuous dispositions, and exercise them whenever an opportunity arises ; being assured that they will gain strength by exercise, as a limb of the body does, and that exercise will make them habitual. From the practice of the purest virtue, you may be assured you will derive the most sublime comforts in every moment of life, and in the moment of death. If ever you find yourself environed with difficulties and perplexing circumstances, out of which you are at a loss how to extricate yourself, do what is right, and be assured that that will extricate

* Peter Carr.

you the best out of the worst situations. Though you cannot see, when you take one step, what will be the next, yet follow truth, justice, and plain dealing, and never fear their leading you out of the labyrinth, in the easiest manner possible. The knot which you thought a Gordian one, will untie itself before you. Nothing is so mistaken as the supposition, that a person is to extricate himself from a difficulty, by intrigue, by chicanery, by dissimulation, by trimming, by an untruth, by an injustice. This increases the difficulties tenfold; and those, who pursue these methods, get themselves so involved at length, that they can turn no way but their infamy becomes more exposed. It is of great importance to set a resolution, not to be shaken, never to tell an untruth. There is no vice so mean, so pitiful, so contemptible; and he who permits himself to tell a lie once, finds it much easier to do it a second and third time, till at length it becomes habitual; he tells lies without attending to it, and truths without the world's believing him. This falsehood of the tongue leads to that of the heart, and in time depraves all its good dispositions.

*   *   *

Moral Philosophy. I think it lost time to attend lectures on this branch. He who made us would have been a pitiful bungler, if he had made the rules of our moral conduct a matter of science. For one man of science, there are thousands who are not. What would have become of them? Man was destined for society. His morality, therefore, was to be formed to this object. He was endowed with a sense of right and wrong, merely relative to this. This sense is as much a part of his nature, as the sense of hearing, seeing, feeling; it is the true foundation of morality, and not τὸ καλόν, truth, &c., as fanciful writers have imagined. The moral sense, or conscience, is as much a part of man as his leg

or arm.   It is given to all human beings in a stronger or
weaker degree, as force of members is given them in a
greater or less degree.   It may be strengthened by exercise, as may any particular limb of the body.   This
sense is submitted, indeed, in some degree, to the guidance of reason ; but it is a small stock which is required
for this : even a less one than what we call common
sense.   State a moral case to a ploughman and a professor.   The former will decide it as well, and often
better than the latter, because he has not been led astray
by artificial rules.   In this branch, therefore, read good
books, because they will encourage, as well as direct
your feelings.   The writings of Sterne, particularly,
form the best course of morality that ever was written.
Besides these, read the books mentioned in the enclosed
paper ; and, above all things, lose no occasion of exercising your dispositions to be grateful, to be generous, to
be charitable, to be humane, to be true, just, firm, orderly, courageous, &c.   Consider every act of this kind,
as an exercise which will strengthen your moral faculties
and increase your worth.

Religion.   Your * reason is now mature enough to
examine this object.   In the first place, divest yourself
of all bias in favor of novelty and singularity of opinion.
Indulge them in any other subject rather than that of
religion.   It is too important, and the consequences of
error may be too serious.   On the other hand, shake off
all the fears and servile prejudices, under which weak
minds are servilely crouched.   Fix reason firmly in her
seat, and call to her tribunal every fact, every opinion.
Question with boldness even the existence of a God ;
because, if there be one, he must more approve of the
homage of reason, than that of blindfolded fear.   You
will naturally examine first, the religion of your own
country.   Read the Bible, then, as you would read
Livy or Tacitus.   Your own reason is the only oracle

* Peter Carr.

given you by heaven, and you are answerable, not for the rightness, but uprightness of the decision.

* * *

The copy of your * Second Thoughts on Instinctive Impulses, with the letter accompanying it, was received just as I was setting out on a journey to this place, two or three days' distant from Monticello. I brought it with me and read it with great satisfaction, and with the more as it contained exactly my own creed on the foundation of morality in man. It is really curious that on a question so fundamental, such a variety of opinions should have prevailed among men, and those, too, of the most exemplary virtue and first order of understanding. It shows how necessary was the care of the Creator in making the moral principle so much a part of our constitution as that no errors of reasoning or of speculation might lead us astray from its observance in practice. Of all the theories on this question, the most whimsical seems to have been that of Wollaston, who considers *truth* as the foundation of morality. Some have made the *love of God* the foundation of morality. This, too, is but a branch of our moral duties, which are generally divided into duties to God and duties to man. If we did a good act merely from the love of God and a belief that it is pleasing to Him, whence arises the morality of the Atheist ? It is idle to say, as some do, that no such being exists.

Self-interest, or rather self-love, or *egoism,* has been more plausibly substituted as the basis of morality. But I consider our relations with others as constituting the boundaries of morality. With ourselves we stand on the ground of identity, not of relation, which last, requiring two subjects, excludes self-love confined to a single one. To ourselves, in strict language, we can owe no duties, obligation requiring also two parties.

* Thomas Law.

Self-love, therefore, is no part of morality. Indeed it is exactly its counterpart. It is the sole antagonist of virtue, leading us constantly by our propensities to self-gratification in violation of our moral duties to others. Accordingly, it is against this enemy that are erected the batteries of moralists and religionists, as the only obstacle to the practice of morality. Take from man his selfish propensities, and he can have nothing to seduce him from the practice of virtue. Or subdue those propensities by education, instruction or restraint, and virtue remains without a competitor. Egoism, in a broader sense, has been thus presented as the source of moral action. It has been said that we feed the hungry, clothe the naked, bind up the wounds of the man beaten by thieves, pour oil and wine into them, set him on our own beast and bring him to the inn, because we receive ourselves pleasure from these acts. So Helvetius, one of the best men on earth, and the most ingenious advocate of this principle, after defining "interest" to mean not merely that which is pecuniary, but whatever may procure us pleasure or withdraw us from pain, says, "the humane man is he to whom the sight of misfortune is insupportable, and who to rescue himself from this spectacle, is forced to succor the unfortunate object." This indeed is true. But it is one step short of the ultimate question. These good acts give us pleasure, but how happens it that they give us pleasure? Because nature hath implanted in our breasts a love of others, a sense of duty to them, a moral instinct, in short, which prompts us irresistibly to feel and to succor their distresses, and protests against the language of Helvetius, "what other motive than self-interest could determine a man to generous actions? It is as impossible for him to love what is good for the sake of good, as to love evil for the sake of evil." The Creator would indeed have been a bungling artist, had he intended man for a social animal, without planting in him social dispositions.

Some have argued against the existence of a moral sense, by saying that if nature had given us such a sense, impelling us to virtuous actions, and warning us against those which are vicious, then nature would also have designated, by some particular ear-marks, the two sets of actions which are, in themselves, the one virtuous and the other vicious. Whereas, we find, in fact, that the same actions are deemed virtuous in one country and vicious in another. The answer is that nature has constituted *utility* to man the standard and best of virtue. Men living in different countries, under different circumstances, different habits and regimens, may have different utilities ; the same act, therefore, may be useful, and consequently virtuous in one country which is injurious and vicious in another differently circumstanced. I sincerely, then, believe with you in the general existence of a moral instinct. I think it the brightest gem with which the human character is studded, and the want of it as more degrading than the most hideous of the bodily deformities.

* * *

But when we come to the moral principles on which the government is to be administered, we come to what is proper for all conditions of society. I meet you * there in all the benevolence and rectitude of your native character ; and I love myself always most where I concur most with you. Liberty, truth, probity, honor, are declared to be the four cardinal principles of your society. I believe with you that morality, compassion, generosity, are innate elements of the human constitution ; that there exists a right independent of force ; that a right to property is founded in our natural wants,

* M. Dupont de Nemours.

in the means with which we are endowed to satisfy these
wants, and the right to what we acquire by those means
without violating the similar rights of other sensible
beings ; that no one has a right to obstruct another, exercising his faculties innocently for the relief of sensibilities made a part of his nature ; that justice is the
fundamental law of society ; that the majority, oppress-
ing an individual, is guilty of a crime, abuses its strength,
and by acting on the law of the strongest breaks up the
foundations of society ; that action by the citizens in
person, in affairs within their reach and competence, and
in all others by representatives, chosen immediately, and
removable by themselves, constitutes the essence of a
republic ; that all governments are more or less republican in proportion as this principle enters more or less
into their composition ; and that a government by
representation is capable of extension over a greater
surface of country than one of any other form.   These,
my friend, are the essentials in which you and I agree ;
however, in our zeal for their maintenance, we may be
perplexed and divaricate, as to the structure of society
most likely to secure them.

at stake

Enlighten the people generally, and tyranny and
oppressions of body and mind will vanish like evil spirits
at the dawn of day.   Although I do not, with some
enthusiasts, believe that the human condition will ever
advance to such a state of perfection as that there shall
no longer be pain or vice in the world, yet I believe it
susceptible of much improvement, and most of all, in
matters of government and religion ; and that the diffusion of knowledge among the people is to be the instrument by which it is to be effected.

*   *   *

To say that gratitude is never to enter into the motives
of national conduct, is to revive a principle which has

been buried for centuries with its kindred principles of the lawfulness of assassination, poison, perjury, &c. All of these were legitimate principles in the dark ages which intervened between ancient and modern civilization, but exploded and held in just horror in the eighteenth century. I know but one code of morality for men, whether acting singly or collectively. He who says I will be a rogue when I act in company with a hundred others, but an honest man when I act alone, will be believed in the former assertion, but not in the latter. I would say with the poet, *"hic niger est, hunc tu Romane cavato."* If the morality of one man produces a just line of conduct in him, acting individually, why should not the morality of one hundred men produce a just line of conduct in them, acting together? But I indulge myself in these reflections, because my own feelings run me into them; with you they were always acknowledged. Let us hope that our new government will take some other occasions to show, that they mean to proscribe no virtue from the canons of their conduct with other nations.

* * *

Our legislators are not sufficiently apprized of the rightful limits of their power; that their true office is to declare and enforce only our natural rights and duties, and to take none of them from us. No man has a natural right to commit aggression on the equal rights of another; and this is all from which the laws ought to restrain him; every man is under the natural duty of contributing to the necessities of the society; and this is all the laws should enforce on him; and, no man having a natural right to be the judge between himself and another, it is his natural duty to submit to the umpirage of an impartial third. When the laws have declared and enforced all this, they have fulfilled their functions;

and the idea is quite unfounded, that on entering into society we give up any natural right.

* * *

He * promises a future work on morals, in which I lament to see that he will adopt the principles of Hobbes, or humiliation to human nature ; that the sense of justice and injustice is not derived from our natural organization, but founded on convention only.   I lament this the more, as he is unquestionably the ablest writer living, on abstract subjects.   Assuming the fact, that the earth has been created in time, and consequently the dogma of final causes, we yield, of course, to this short syllogism.   Man was created for social intercourse ; but social intercourse cannot be maintained without a sense of justice ; then man must have been created with a sense of justice.

* * *

This work, which is on Ethics, I have not seen, but suspect I shall differ from it in its foundation, although not in its deductions.   I gather from his other works that he adopts the principle of Hobbes, that justice is founded in contract solely, and does not result from the construction of man.   I believe, on the contrary, that it is instinct and innate, that the moral sense is as much a part of our constitution as that of feeling, seeing, or hearing ; as a wise creator must have seen to be necessary in an animal destined to live in society ; that every human mind feels pleasure in doing good to another ; that the non-existence of justice is not to be inferred from the fact that the same act is deemed virtuous and right in one society which is held vicious and wrong in another ; because, as the circumstances and opinions of different societies vary, so the acts which may do them right or wrong must vary also ; for virtue does not con-

* Destutt Tracy.

sist in the act we do, but in the end it is to effect. If it is to effect the happiness of him to whom it is directed, it is virtuous, while in a society under different circumstances and opinions, the same act might produce pain, and would be vicious. The essence of virtue is in doing good to others, while what is good may be one thing in one society, and its contrary in another.

* * *

As to myself, my religious reading has long been confined to the moral branch of religion, which is the same in all religions , while in that branch which consists of dogmas, all differ, all have a different set. The former instructs us how to live well and worthily in society ; the latter are made to interest our minds in the support of the teachers who inculcate them. Hence, for one sermon on a moral subject, you hear ten on the dogmas of the sect. However, religion is not the subject for you * and me ; neither of us know the religious opinions of the other ; that is a matter between our Maker and ourselves.

* * *

Reading, reflection and time have convinced me that the interests of society require the observation of those moral precepts only in which all religions agree, (for all forbid us to murder, steal, plunder, or bear false witness,) and that we should not intermeddle with the particular dogmas in which all religions differ, and which are totally unconnected with morality. In all of them we see good men, and as many in one as another. The varieties in the structure and action of the human mind as in those of the body, are the work of our Creator, against which it cannot be a religious duty to erect the standard of uniformity. The practice of morality being necessary for the well-being of society, he has taken care

* Thomas Leiper.

to impress its precepts so indelibly on our hearts that they shall not be effaced by the subtleties of our brain. We all agree in the obligation of the moral precepts of Jesus, and nowhere will they be found delivered in greater purity than in his discourses.

* * *

An eloquent preacher of your * religious society, Richard Motte, in a discourse of much emotion and pathos, is said to have exclaimed aloud to his congregation, that he did not believe there was a Quaker, Presbyterian, Methodist or Baptist in heaven, having paused to give his hearers time to stare and to wonder. He added, that in heaven, God knew no distinctions, but considered all good men as his children, and as brethren of the same family. I believe, with the Quaker preacher, that he who steadily observes those moral precepts in which all religions concur, will never be questioned at the gates of heaven, as to the dogmas in which they all differ. That on entering there, all these are left behind us, and the Aristides and Catos, the Penns and Tillotsons, Presbyterians and Baptists, will find themselves united in all principles which are in concert with the reason of the supreme mind. Of all the systems of morality, ancient or modern, which have come under my observation, none appear to me so pure as that of Jesus. He who follows this steadily need not, I think, be uneasy, although he cannot comprehend the subtleties and mysteries erected on his doctrines by those who, calling themselves his special followers and favorites, would make him come into the world to lay snares for all understandings but theirs.

* * *

In the New Testament there is internal evidence that parts of it have proceeded from an extraordinary man ;

* William Canby.

and that other parts are of the fabric of very inferior minds. It is as easy to separate those parts, as to pick out diamonds from dunghills. The matter of the first was such as would be preserved in the memory of the hearers, and handed on by tradition for a long time ; the latter such stuff as might be gathered up, for imbedding it, anywhere, and at any time.

* * *

I have trust in him who made us what we are, and know it was not his plan to make us always unerring. IIe has formed us moral agents. Not that, in the perfection of his state, he can feel pain or pleasure in anything we may do ; he is far above our power ; but that we may promote the happiness of those with whom he has placed us in society, by acting honestly towards all, benevolently to those who fall within our way, respecting sacredly their rights, bodily and mental, and cherishing especially their freedom of conscience, as we value our own. I must ever believe that religion substantially good which produces an honest life, and we have been authorized by one whom you and I equally respect, to judge of the tree by its fruit. Our particular principles of religion are a subject of accountability to our God alone. I inquire after no man's, and trouble none with mine ; nor is it given to us in this life to know whether yours or mine, our friends or our foes, are exactly the right.

* * *

I, too, have made a wee-little book from the same materials, which I call the Philosophy of Jesus ; it is a paradigma of his doctrines, made by cutting the texts out of the book, and arranging them on the pages of a blank book, in a certain order of time or subject. A more beautiful or precious morsel of ethics I have never seen ; it is a document in proof that *I* am a *real Christian,* that is to say, a disciple of the doctrines of Jesus, very different from the Platonists, who call *me* infidel and *themselves* Christians and preachers of the gospel, while they draw all their characteristic dogmas from what its author never said nor saw. They have compounded from the heathen mysteries a system beyond the comprehension of man, of which the great reformer of the vicious ethics and deism of the Jews, were he to return to earth, would not recognize one feature.

* * *

In that branch of religion which regards the moralities of life, and the duties of a social being, which teaches us to love our neighbors as ourselves, and to do good to all men, I am sure that you * and I do not differ. We probably differ on the dogmas of theology, the foundation of all sectarianism, and on which no two sects dream alike ; for if they did they would then be of the same. You say you are a Calvinist. I am not. I am of a sect by myself, as far as I know. I am not a Jew, and therefore do not adopt their theology, which supposes the God of infinite justice to punish the sins of the fathers upon their children, unto the third and fourth generation ; and the benevolent and sublime reformer of that religion has told us only that God is good and perfect, but has not defined him. I am, therefore, of his theology, believing that we have neither words nor ideas adequate to that definition. And if we could all, after this example, leave the subject as undefinable, we should all be of one sect, doers of good, and eschewers of evil. No doctrines of his lead to schism. It is the speculations of crazy theologists which have made a Babel of a religion the most moral and sublime ever preached to man, and calculated to heal, and not to create differences. These religious animosities I impute to those who call themselves his ministers, and who engraft their

* Ezra Styles.

evidence of God w/ intricate design of the World (handwritten annotation)

casuistries on the stock of his simple precepts.   I am sometimes more angry with them than is authorized by the blessed charities which he preaches.

* * *

In our * university you † know there is no Professor-ship of Divinity.   A handle has been made of this, to disseminate an idea that this is an institution, not merely of no religion, but against all religion.   We suggest the expediency of encouraging the different religious sects to establish, each for itself, a professorship of their own tenets, on the confines of the university, so near as that their students may attend the lectures there, and have the free use of our library, and every other accommoda-tion we can give them ; preserving, however, their in-dependence of us and of each other.   This fills the chasm objected to ours, as a defect in an institution pro-fessing to give instruction in *all* useful sciences.   I think the invitation will be accepted, by some sects from candid intentions, and by others from jealousy and rival-ship.   And by bringing the sects together, and mixing them with the mass of other students, we shall soften their asperities, liberalize and neutralize their prejudices, and make the general religion a religion of peace, rea-son, and morality.

* * *

I hold, (without appeal to revelation) that when we take a view of the universe, in its parts, general or par-ticular, it is impossible for the human mind not to per-ceive and feel a conviction of design, consummate skill, and indefinite power in every atom of its composition. The movements of the heavenly bodies, so exactly held in their course by the balance of centrifugal and cen-tripetal forces ; the structure of our earth itself, with its

* University of Virginia.
† Dr. Thomas Cooper.

distribution of lands, waters and atmosphere ; animal and vegetable bodies, examined in all their minutest particles ; insects, mere atoms of life, yet as perfectly organized as man or mammoth ; the mineral substances, their generation and uses ; it is impossible, I say, for the human mind not to believe, that there is in all this, design, cause and effect, up to an ultimate cause, a fabricator of all things from matter and motion, their preserver and regulator while permitted to exist in their present forms, and their regeneration into new and other forms. We see, too, evident proofs of the necessity of a superintending power, to maintain the universe in its course and order.

* * *

In consequence of some conversation with Dr. Rush,* in the year 1798–99, I had promised some day to write him a letter giving him my view of the Christian system. I have reflected often on it since, and even sketched the outlines in my own mind. I should first take a general view of the moral doctrines of the most remarkable of the ancient philosophers, of whose ethics we have sufficient information to make an estimate, say Pythagoras, Epicurus, Epictetus, Socrates, Cicero, Seneca, Antoninus. I should do justice to the branches of morality they have treated well ; but point out the importance of those in which they are deficient. I should then take a view of the deism and ethics of the Jews, and show in what a degraded state they were, and the necessity they presented of a reformation. I should proceed to a view of the life, character, and doctrines of Jesus, who sensible of incorrectness of their ideas of the Deity, and of morality, endeavored to bring them to the principles of a pure deism, and juster notions of the attributes of God, to reform their moral doctrines to the standard of reason, justice and philanthropy, and to inculcate the belief of a future state. This view would purposely

* Dr. Benjamin Rush.

omit the question of his divinity, and even his inspiration. To do him justice, it would be necessary to remark the disadvantages his doctrines had to encounter, not having been committed to writing by himself, but by the most unlettered of men, by memory, long after they had heard them from him ; when much was forgotten, much misunderstood, and presented in every paradoxical shape. Yet such are the fragments remaining as to show a master workman, and that his system of morality was the most benevolent and sublime probably that has been ever taught, and consequently more perfect than those of any of the ancient philosophers.

* * *

The morality of Jesus, as taught by himself, and freed from the corruptions of latter times, is far superior. Their philosophy went chiefly to the government of our passions, so far as respected ourselves, and the procuring our own tranquillity. In our duties to others they were short and deficient. They extended their cares scarcely beyond our kindred and friends individually, and our country in the abstract. Jesus embraced with charity and philanthropy our neighbors, our countrymen, and the whole family of mankind. They confined themselves to actions ; he pressed his sentiments into the region of our thoughts, and called for purity at the fountain head.

I never will, by any word or act, bow to the shrine of intolerance, or admit a right of inquiry into the religious opinions of others. On the contrary, we are bound, you,* I, and every one, to make common cause, even with error itself, to maintain the common right of freedom of conscience. We ought with one heart and one hand to hew down the daring and dangerous efforts of those who would seduce the public opinion to substitute itself into that tyranny over religious faith which the laws have so justly abdicated.

* Edward Dowse.

INTELLECTUAL FREEDOM AND
PROGRESS

I have sworn upon the altar of God, eternal hostility against every form of tyranny over the mind of man. But this is all they * have to fear from me : and enough too in their opinion.

*   *   *

This is a summary view of that religious slavery under which a people have been willing to remain, who have lavished their lives and fortunes for the establishment of their civil freedom. The error seems not sufficiently eradicated, that the operations of the mind, as well as the acts of the body, are subject to the coercion of the laws. But our rulers can have no authority over such natural rights, only as we have submitted to them. The rights of conscience we never submitted, we could not submit. We are answerable for them to our God. The legitimate powers of government extend to such acts only as are injurious to others. But it does me no injury for my neighbor to say there are twenty gods, or no God. It neither picks my pocket nor breaks my leg. If it be said, his testimony in a court of justice cannot be relied on, reject it then, and be the stigma on him. Constraint may make him worse by making him a hypocrite, but it will never make him a truer man. It may fix him obstinately in his errors, but will not cure them. Reason and free inquiry are the only effectual agents against error. Give a loose to them, they will support the true religion by bringing every false one to their tribunal, to the test of their investigation. They are the natural enemies of error, and of error only. Had not the Roman government permitted free inquiry, Christianity could never have been introduced. Had

* Religious sects.

not free inquiry been indulged at the era of the reformation, the corruptions of Christianity could not have
been purged away. If it be restrained now, the present
corruptions will be protected, and new ones encouraged.
Was the government to prescribe to us our medicine
and diet, our bodies would be in such keeping as our
souls are now. Thus in France the emetic was once
forbidden as a medicine, and the potato as an article
of food. Government is just as infallible, too, when it
fixes systems in physics. Galileo was sent to the Inquisition for affirming that the earth was a sphere; the
government had declared it to be as flat as a trencher,
and Galileo was obliged to abjure his error. This error,
however, at length prevailed, the earth became a globe,
and Descartes declared it was whirled round its axis by
a vortex. The government in which he lived was wise
enough to see that this was no question of civil jurisdiction, or we should all have been involved by authority
in vortices. In fact, the vortices have been exploded,
and the Newtonian principle of gravitation is now more
firmly established, on the basis of reason, than it would
be were the government to step in, and to make it an
article of necessary faith. Reason and experiment have
been indulged, and error has fled before them. It is
error alone which needs the support of government.
Truth can stand by itself. Subject opinion to coercion: whom will you make your inquisitors? Fallible
men; men governed by bad passions, by private as well
as public reasons. And why subject it to coercion?
To produce uniformity. But is uniformity of opinion
desirable? No more than of face and stature. Introduce the bed of Procrustes then, and as there is danger
that the large men may beat the small, make us all of a
size, by lopping the former and stretching the latter.
Difference of opinion is advantageous in religion. The
several sects perform the office of a *censor morum* over
each other. Is uniformity attainable? Millions of in-

nocent men, women, and children, since the introduction of Christianity, have been burnt, tortured, fined, imprisoned ; yet we have not advanced one inch towards uniformity. What has been the effect of coercion ? To make one half the world fools, and the other half hypocrites. To support roguery and error all over the earth. Let us reflect that it is inhabited by a thousand millions of people. That these profess probably a thousand different systems of religion. That ours is but one of that thousand. That if there be but one right, and ours that one, we should wish to see the nine hundred and ninety-nine wandering sects gathered into the fold of truth. But against such a majority we cannot effect this by force. Reason and persuasion are the only practicable instruments. To make way for these, free inquiry must be indulged ; and how can we wish others to indulge it while we refuse it ourselves.

* * *

An Act for establishing Religious Freedom, passed in the Assembly of Virginia in the beginning of the year 1786.

Well aware that Almighty God hath created the mind free ; that all attempts to influence it by temporal punishments or burdens, or by civil incapacitations, tend only to beget habits of hypocrisy and meanness, and are a departure from the plan of the Holy Author of our religion, who being Lord both of body and mind, yet chose not to propagate it by coercions on either, as was in his Almighty power to do ; that the impious presumption of legislators and rulers, civil as well as ecclesiastical, who, being themselves but fallible and uninspired men have assumed dominion over the faith of others, setting up their own opinions and modes of thinking as the only true and infallible, and as such endeavoring to impose them on others, hath established and maintained false religions over the greatest part of the world, and through all time ; that to compel a man to furnish contributions of money for the propagation of opinions which he disbelieves, is sinful and tyrannical ; that even the forcing him to support this or that teacher of his own religious persuasion, is depriving him of the comfortable liberty of giving his contributions to the particular pastor whose morals he would make his pattern, and whose powers he feels most persuasive to righteousness, and is withdrawing from the ministry those temporal rewards, which proceeding from an approbation of their personal conduct, are an additional incitement to earnest and unremitting labors for the instruction of mankind ; that our civil rights have no dependence on our religious opinions, more than our opinions in physics or geometry ; that, therefore, the proscribing any citizen as unworthy the public confidence by laying upon him an incapacity of being called to the offices of trust and emolument, unless he profess or renounce this or that religious opinion, is depriving him injuriously of those privileges and advantages to which in common with his fellow citizens he has a natural right ; that it tends also to corrupt the principles of that very religion it is meant to encourage, by bribing, with a monopoly of worldly honors and emoluments, those who will externally profess and conform to it ; that though indeed these are criminal who do not withstand such temptation, yet neither are those innocent who lay the bait in their way ; that to suffer the civil magistrate to intrude his powers into the field of opinion and to restrain the profession or propagation of principles, on the supposition of their ill tendency, is a dangerous fallacy, which at once destroys all religious liberty, because he being of course judge of that tendency, will make his opinions the rule of judgment, and approve or condemn the sentiments of others only as they shall square with or differ from his own ; that it is time enough for the rightful purposes of civil government, for its officers to interfere when principles break out into overt acts against peace and good order ; and finally, that truth is great and will prevail if left to herself, that she is the proper and sufficient antagonist to error, and has nothing to fear from the conflict, unless by human interposition disarmed of her natural weapons, free argument and debate, errors ceasing to be dangerous when it is permitted freely to contradict them.

Be it therefore enacted by the General Assembly, That no man shall be compelled to frequent or support any religious worship, place or ministry whatsoever, nor shall be enforced, restrained, molested, or burthened in his body or goods, nor shall otherwise suffer on account of his religious opinions or belief ; but that all men shall be free to profess, and by argument to maintain, their opinions in matters of religion, and that the same shall in nowise diminish, enlarge, or affect their civil capacities.

We are free to declare, and do declare, that the rights hereby asserted are of the natural rights of mankind, and that if any act shall be hereafter passed to repeal the present or to narrow its operation, such act will be an infringement of natural right.

* * *

Believing with you * that religion is a matter which lies solely between man and his God, that he owes account to none other for his faith or his worship, that the legislative powers of government reach actions only, and not opinions, I contemplate with sovereign reverence that act of the whole American people which declared that their legislature should "make no law respecting an establishment of religion, or prohibiting the free exercise thereof," thus building a wall of separation

* Danbury Baptist Association, Conn.

between church and State. Adhering to this expression
of the supreme will of the nation in behalf of the rights
of conscience, I shall see with sincere satisfaction the
progress of those sentiments which tend to restore to
man all his natural rights, convinced he has no natural
right in opposition to his social duties.

* * *

In reviewing the history of the times through which
we have past, no portion of it gives greater satisfaction,
on reflection, than that which presents the efforts of
the friends of religious freedom, and the success with
which they were crowned. We have solved by fair
experiment, the great and interesting question whether
freedom of religion is compatible with order in government, and obedience to the laws. And we have experienced the quiet as well as the comfort which results
from leaving every one to profess freely and openly
those principles of religion which are the inductions of
his own reason, and the serious convictions of his own
inquiries.

* * *

The Virginia act for religious freedom has been received with infinite approbation in Europe, and propagated with enthusiasm. I do not mean by the governments, but by the individuals who compose them. It
has been translated into French and Italian, has been sent
to most of the courts of Europe, and has been the best
evidence of the falsehood of those reports which stated
us to be in anarchy. It is inserted in the new Ency-
clopedie, and is appearing in most of the publications
respecting America. In fact, it is comfortable to see
the standard of reason at length erected, after so many
ages, during which the human mind has been held in
vassalage by kings, priests, and nobles ; and it is honorable for us, to have produced the first legislature who

had the courage to declare, that the reason of man may be trusted with the formation of his own opinions.

bem progress

* * *

What an effort, my dear Sir,* of bigotry in politics and religion have we gone through! The barbarians really flattered themselves they should be able to bring back the times of Vandalism, when ignorance put everything into the hands of power and priestcraft. All advances in science were proscribed as innovations. They pretended to praise and encourage education, but it was to be the education of our ancestors. We were to look backwards, not forwards, for improvement; the President himself declaring, in one of his answers to addresses, that we were never to expect to go beyond them in real science. This was the real ground of all the attacks on you. Those who live by mystery and *charlatanerie,* fearing you would render them useless by simplifying the Christian philosophy, — the most sublime and benevolent, but most perverted system that ever shone on man, — endeavored to crush your well-earned and well-deserved fame. But it was the Lilliputians upon Gulliver. Our countrymen have recovered from the alarm into which art and industry had thrown them; science and honesty are replaced on their high ground. We can no longer say there is nothing new under the sun. For this whole chapter in the history of man is new. The great extent of our Republic is new. Its sparse habitation is new. The mighty wave of public opinion which has rolled over it is new. But the most pleasing novelty is, its so quietly subsiding over such an extent of surface to its true level again. The order and good sense displayed in this recovery from delusion, and in the momentous crisis which lately arose, really bespeak a strength of character in our nation which augurs well for the duration of our Re-

* Dr. Joseph Priestley.

public ; and I am much better satisfied now of its stability than I was before it was tried.

* * *

But the endeavors to enlighten them on the fate which awaits their present course of life, to induce them to exercise their reason, follow its dictates, and change their pursuits with the change of circumstances, have powerful obstacles to encounter ; they are combated by the habits of their bodies, prejudice of their minds, ignorance, pride, and the influence of interested and crafty individuals among them, who feel themselves something in the present order of things, and fear to become nothing in any other. These persons inculcate a sanctimonious reverence for the customs of their ancestors ; that whatsoever they did, must be done through all time ; that reason is a false guide, and to advance under its counsel, in their physical, moral, or political condition, is perilous innovation ; that their duty is to remain as their Creator made them, ignorance being safety, and knowledge full of danger ; in short, my friends, among them is seen the action and counteraction of good sense and bigotry ; they, too, have their anti-philosophers, who find an interest in keeping things in their present state, who dread reformation, and exert all their faculties to maintain the ascendency of habit over the duty of improving our reason, and obeying its mandates.

* * *

It is a proper topic, not only to promote the work of humanizing our citizens towards the Indians, but to conciliate to us the good opinion of Europe on the subject of them. This, however, might have been done in half the compass it here occupies. But every respecter of science, every friend to political reformation, must have observed with indignation the hue and cry raised against philosophy and the rights of man ; and it really seems as if they would be overborne, and barbarism, bigotry, and despotism, would recover the ground they have lost by the advance of the public understanding. I have thought the occasion justified some discountenance of these anti-social doctrines, some testimony against them. But not to commit myself in direct warfare on them, I have thought it best to say what is directly applied to the Indians only, but admits by inference a more general extension.

* * *

In every country where man is free to think and to speak, differences of opinion will arise from difference of perception, and the imperfection of reason ; but these differences when permitted, as in this happy country, to purify themselves by free discussion, are but as passing clouds overspreading our land transiently, and leaving our horizon more bright and serene.

* * *

I am sensible how far I should fall short of effecting all the reformation which reason would suggest, and experience approve, were I free to do whatever I thought best ; but when we reflect how difficult it is to move or inflect the great machine of society, how impossible to advance the notions of a whole people suddenly to ideal right, we see the wisdom of Solon's remark, that no more good must be attempted than the nation can bear.

* * *

No experiment can be more interesting than that we are now trying, and which we trust will end in establishing the fact, that man may be governed by reason and truth. Our first object should therefore be, to leave open to him all the avenues to truth. The most effectual hitherto found, is the freedom of the press.

Freedom of press

It is therefore, the first shut up by those who fear the
investigation of their actions. The firmness with which
the people have withstood the late abuses of the press,
the discernment they have manifested between truth
and falsehood, show that they may safely be trusted to
hear everything true and false, and to form a correct
judgment between them. As little is it necessary to
impose on their senses, or dazzle their minds by pomp,
splendor, or forms. Instead of this artificial, how much
surer is that real respect, which results from the use of
their reason, and the habit of bringing everything to the
test of common sense.

I hold it, therefore, certain, that to open the doors
of truth, and to fortify the habit of testing everything
by reason, are the most effectual manacles we can rivet
on the hands of our successors to prevent their mana-
cling the people with their own consent.

* * *

It is a melancholy truth, that a suppression of the
press could not more completely deprive the nation of
its benefits, than is done by its abandoned prostitution
to falsehood. Nothing can now be believed which is
seen in a newspaper. Truth itself becomes suspicious
by being put into that polluted vehicle. The real extent of this state of misinformation is known only to
those who are in situations to confront facts within their
knowledge with the lies of the day. I really look with
commiseration over the great body of my fellow citizens, who, reading newspapers, live and die in the belief, that they have known something of what has been
passing in the world in their time ; whereas the accounts
they have read in newspapers are just as true a history
of any other period of the world as of the present,
except that the real names of the day are affixed to
their fables.

Perhaps an editor might begin a reformation in some

such way as this. Divide his paper into four chapters, heading the 1st, Truths. 2d, Probabilities. 3d, Possibilities. 4th, Lies. The first chapter would be very short, as it would contain little more than authentic papers, and information from such sources, as the editor would be willing to risk his own reputation for their truth. The second would contain what, from a mature consideration of all circumstances, his judgment should conclude to be probably true. This, however, should rather contain too little than too much. The third and fourth should be professedly for those readers who would rather have lies for their money than the blank paper they would occupy.

Such an editor too, would have to set his face against the demoralising practice of feeding the public mind habitually on slander, and the depravity of taste which this nauseous aliment induces. Defamation is becoming a necessary of life ; insomuch, that a dish of tea in the morning or evening cannot be digested without this stimulant. Even those who do not believe these abominations, still read them with complaisance to their auditors, and instead of the abhorrence and indignation which should fill a virtuous mind, betray a secret pleasure in the possibility that some may believe them, though they do not themselves. It seems to escape them, that it is not he who prints, but he who pays for printing a slander, who is its real author.

* * *

There is a snail-paced gate for the advance of new ideas on the general mind, under which we must acquiesce. A forty years' experience of popular assemblies has taught me, that you must give them time for every step you take. If too hard pushed, they baulk, and the machine retrogrades.

* * *

But even in Europe a change has sensibly taken place in the mind of man. Science had liberated the ideas of those who read and reflect, and the American example had kindled feelings of right in the people. An insurrection has consequently begun, of science, talents, and courage, against rank and birth, which have fallen into contempt. It has failed in its first effort, because the mobs of the cities, the instrument used for its accomplishment, debased by ignorance, poverty, and vice, could not be restrained to rational action. But the world will recover from the panic of this first catastrophe. Science is progressive, and talents and enterprise on the alert. Resort may be had to the people of the country, a more governable power from their principles and subordination ; and rank, and birth, and tinsel-aristocracy will finally shrink into insignificance, even there. This, however, we have no right to meddle with. It suffices for us, if the moral and physical condition of our own citizens qualifies them to select the able and good for the direction of their government, with a recurrence of elections at such short periods as will enable them to displace an unfaithful servant, before the mischief he meditates may be irremediable.

* * *

Is this then our freedom of religion ? and are we to have a censor whose imprimatur shall say what books may be sold, and what we may buy ? And who is thus to dogmatize religious opinions for our citizens ? Whose foot is to be the measure to which ours are all to be cut or stretched ? Is a priest to be our inquisitor, or shall a layman, simple as ourselves, set up his reason as the rule for what we are to read, and what we must believe ? It is an insult to our citizens to question whether they are rational beings or not, and blasphemy against religion to suppose it cannot stand the test of truth and reason. If M. de Becourt's book be false in its facts, disprove them ; if false in its reasoning, refute it.   But, for God's sake, let us freely hear both sides, if we choose.   I know little of its contents, having barely glanced over here and there a passage, and over the table of contents.   From this, the Newtonian philosophy seemed the chief object of attack, the issue of which might be trusted to the strength of the two combatants ; Newton certainly not needing the auxiliary arm of the government, and still less the holy author of our religion, as to what in it concerns him.   I thought the work would be very innocent, and one which might be confided to the reason of any man ; not likely to be much read if let alone, but, if persecuted, it will be generally read.   Every man in the United States will think it a duty to buy a copy, in vindication of his right to buy, and to read what he pleases.

* * *

If a nation expects to be ignorant and free, in a state of civilization, it expects what never was and never will be.   The functionaries of every government have propensities to command at will the liberty and property of their constituents.   There is no safe deposit for these but with the people themselves ; nor can they be safe with them without information.   Where the press is free, and every man able to read, all is safe.

* * *

Bigotry is the disease of ignorance, of morbid minds, enthusiasm of the free and buoyant.   Education and free discussion are the antidotes of both.   We are destined to be a barrier against the returns of ignorance and barbarism.   Old Europe will have to lean on our shoulders, and to hobble along by our side, under the monkish trammels of priests and kings, as she can.   What a colossus shall we be when the southern continent comes up to our mark !   What a stand will it secure as a

ralliance for the reason and freedom of the globe ! I
like the dreams of the future better than the history of
the past, — so good night !

* * *

The amendments of which we have as yet heard,
prove the advance of liberalism in the intervening
period ; and encourage a hope that the human mind
will some day get back to the freedom it enjoyed two
thousand years ago. This country, which has given
to the world the example of physical liberty, owes to
it that of moral emancipation also, for as yet it is but
nominal with us. The inquisition of public opinion
overwhelms in practice, the freedom asserted by the
laws in theory.

* * *

I shall not die without a hope that light and liberty
are on steady advance. We have seen, indeed, once
within the records of history, a complete eclipse of the
human mind continuing for centuries. And this, too,
by swarms of the same northern barbarians, conquering
and taking possession of the countries and governments
of the civilized world. Should this be again attempted,
should the same northern hordes, allured again by the
corn, wine, and oil of the south, be able again to settle
their swarms in the countries of their growth, the art
of printing alone, and the vast dissemination of books,
will maintain the mind where it is, and raise the conquering ruffians to the level of the conquered, instead of
degrading these to that of their conquerors. And even
should the cloud of barbarism and despotism again ob-
scure the science and liberties of Europe, this country
remains to preserve and restore light and liberty to them.
In short, the flames kindled on the 4th of July, 1776,
have spread over too much of the globe to be extinguished by the feeble engines of despotism ; on the

contrary, they will consume these engines and all who work them.

* * *

Science is more important in a republican than in any other government.   And in an infant country like ours, we must much depend for improvement on the science of other countries, longer established, possessing better means, and more advanced than we are.   To prohibit us from the benefit of foreign light, is to consign us to long darkness.

* * *

I look to the diffusion of light and education as the resource most to be relied on for ameliorating the condition, promoting the virtue, and advancing the happiness of man.   That every man shall be made virtuous, by any process whatever, is, indeed, no more to be expected, than that every tree shall be made to bear fruit, and every plant nourishment.   The brier and bramble can never become the vine and olive ; but their asperities may be softened by culture, and their properties improved to usefulness in the order and economy of the world.   And I do hope that, in the present spirit of extending to the great mass of mankind the blessings of instruction, I see a prospect of great advancement in the happiness of the human race ; and that this may proceed to an indefinite, although not to an infinite degree.

* * *   / army: protect govt./ country

I am persuaded myself that the good sense of the people will always be found to be the best army.   They may be led astray for a moment, but will soon correct themselves.   The people are the only censors of their governors ; and even their errors will tend to keep these to the true principles of their institution.   To punish these errors too severely would be to suppress the only

check gov

safeguard of the public liberty. The way to prevent
these irregular interpositions of the people, is to give
them full information of their affairs through the channel of the public papers, and to contrive that those
papers should penetrate the whole mass of the people.
The basis of our governments being the opinion of the
people, the very first object should be to keep that right ;
and were it left to me to decide whether we should have
a government without newspapers, or newspapers without a government, I should not hesitate a moment to
prefer the latter. But I should mean that every man
should receive those papers, and be capable of reading
them. I am convinced that those societies (as the Indians) which live without government, enjoy in their
general mass an infinitely greater degree of happiness
than those who live under the European governments.
Among the former, public opinion is in the place of
law, and restrains morals as powerfully as laws ever did
anywhere. Among the latter, under pretence of governing, they have divided their nations into two classes,
wolves and sheep. I do not exaggerate. This is a true
picture of Europe. Cherish, therefore, the spirit of our
people, and keep alive their attention. Do not be too
severe upon their errors, but reclaim them by enlighten-
ing them. If once they become inattentive to the public
affairs, you * and I, and Congress and Assemblies, Judges
and Governors, shall all become wolves. It seems to
be the law of our general nature, in spite of individual
exceptions ; and experience declares that man is the only
animal which devours his own kind ; for I can apply no
milder term to the governments of Europe, and to the
general prey of the rich on the poor.

*   *   *

As to myself, conscious that there was not a *truth* on
earth which I feared should be known, I have lent my-

* Colonel Edward Carrington.

self willingly as the subject of a great experiment, which was to prove that an administration, conducting itself with integrity and common understanding, cannot be battered down, even by the falsehoods of a licentious press, and consequently still less by the press, as restrained within the legal and wholesome limits of truth. This experiment was wanting for the world to demonstrate the falsehood of the pretext that freedom of the press is incompatible with orderly government. I have never therefore even contradicted the thousands of calumnies so industriously propagated against myself. But the fact being once established, that the press is impotent when it abandons itself to falsehood, I leave to others to restore it to its strength, by recalling it within the pale of truth. Within that it is a noble institution, equally the friend of science and of civil liberty. If this can once be effected in your State, I trust we shall soon see its citizens rally to the republican principles of our Constitution, which unite their sister-States into one family. It would seem impossible that an intelligent people, with the faculty of reading and right of thinking, should continue much longer to slumber under the pupilage of an interested aristocracy of priests and lawyers, persuading them to distrust themselves, and to let them think for them.

* * *

During this course of administration, and in order to disturb it, the artillery of the press has been levelled against us, charged with whatsoever its licentiousness could devise or dare. These abuses of an institution so important to freedom and science, are deeply to be regretted, inasmuch as they tend to lessen its usefulness, and to sap its safety. The offenders have therefore been left to find their punishment in the public indignation.

Nor was it uninteresting to the world, that an experiment should be fairly and fully made, whether freedom of discussion, unaided by power, is not sufficient for the propagation and protection of truth — whether a government, conducting itself in the true spirit of its constitution, with zeal and purity, and doing no act which it would be unwilling the whole world should witness, can be written down by falsehood and defamation.

* * *

Resolved, That it is true as a general principle, and is also expressly declared by one of the amendments to the Constitution, that "the powers not delegated to the United States by the Constitution, nor prohibited by it to the States, are reserved to the States respectively, or to the people ;" and that no power over the freedom of religion, freedom of speech, or freedom of the press being delegated to the United States by the Constitution, nor prohibited by it to the States, all lawful powers respecting the same did of right remain, and were reserved to the States or the people : that thus was manifested their determination to retain to themselves the right of judging how far the licentiousness of speech and of the press may be abridged without lessening their useful freedom, and how far those abuses which cannot be separated from their use should be tolerated, rather than the use be destroyed. And thus also they guarded against all abridgment by the United States of the freedom of religious opinions and exercises, and retained to themselves the right of protecting the same, as this State, by a law passed on the general demand of its citizens, had already protected them from all human restraint or interference. And that in addition to this general principle and express declaration, another and more special provision has been made by one of the amendments to the Constitution, which expressly declares, that "Congress shall make no law respecting an establishment of religion, or prohibiting the free exercise thereof, or abridging the freedom of speech or of the press :"

thereby guarding in the same sentence, and under the same words, the freedom of religion, of speech, and of the press : insomuch, that whatever violated either, throws down the sanctuary which covers the others, and that libels, falsehood, and defamation, equally with heresy and false religion, are withheld from the cognizance of federal tribunals. That, therefore, the act of Congress of the United States, passed on the 14th day of July, 1798, intituled "An Act in addition to the act intituled An Act for the punishment of certain crimes against the United States," which does abridge the freedom of the press, is not law, but is altogether void, and of no force.

* * *

It excites the gratifying reflection that my own country has been the first to prove to the world two truths, that man can govern himself, and that religious freedom is the most effectual anode against religious dissension. I am happy in the restoration of the Jews particularly to their social rights.

* * *

EDUCATION

We thought that on this subject, a systematical plan of general education should be proposed, and I was requested to undertake it. I accordingly prepared three bills for the Revisal, proposing three distinct grades of education, reaching all classes. 1st. Elementary schools, for all children generally, rich and poor. 2d. Colleges, for a middle degree of instruction, calculated for the common purposes of life, and such as would be desirable for all who were in easy circumstances. And, 3d, an ultimate grade for teaching the sciences generally, and in their highest degree. The first bill proposed to lay off every county into Hundreds, or Wards, of a proper size and population for a school, in which reading, writing, and common arithmetic should be taught ; and that the whole State should be divided into twenty-four districts, in each of which should be a school for classical learning, grammar, geography, and the higher branches of numerical arithmetic. The second bill proposed to amend the constitution of William and Mary college, to enlarge its sphere of science, and to make it in fact a University. The third was for the establishment of a library. These bills were not acted on until the same year, '96, and then only so much of the first as provided for elementary schools. And in the Elementary bill, they inserted a provision which completely defeated it ; for they left it to the court of each county to determine for itself, when this act should be carried into execution, within their county. One provision of the bill was, that the expenses of these schools should be borne by the inhabitants of the county, every one in proportion to his general tax rate. This would throw on wealth the education of the poor ; and the justices, being generally of the more wealthy class, were unwilling to incur that burden, and I believe it was not suffered to commence in a single county.

* * *

Another object of the revisal is, to diffuse knowledge more generally through the mass of the people. This bill proposes to lay off every county into small districts of five or six miles square, called hundreds, and in each of them to establish a school for teaching, reading, writing, and arithmetic. The tutor to be supported by the hundred, and every person in it entitled to send their children three years gratis, and as much longer as they please, paying for it. These schools to be under a visitor who is annually to choose the boy of best genius in the school, of those whose parents are too poor to give them further education, and to send him forward to one of the grammar schools, of which twenty are proposed to be erected in different parts of the country, for teaching Greek, Latin, Geography, and the higher branches of numerical arithmetic. Of the boys thus sent in one year, trial is to be made at the grammar schools one or two years, and the best genius of the whole selected, and continued six years, and the residue dismissed. By this means twenty of the best geniuses will be raked from the rubbish annually, and be instructed, at the public expense, so far as the grammar schools go. At the end of six years instruction, one half are to be discontinued (from among whom the grammar schools will probably be supplied with future masters) ; and the other half, who are to be chosen for the superiority of their parts and disposition, are to be sent and continued three years in the study of such sciences as they shall choose, at William and Mary college, the plan of which is proposed to be enlarged, as will be hereafter explained, and extended to all the useful sciences. The ultimate result of the whole scheme of education would be the teaching all the children of the State reading, writing, and common arithmetic ; turning out ten annually, of superior genius, well taught in Greek, Latin, Geography, and the higher branches of arithmetic ; turning out ten others annually, of still superior parts, who, to those branches of learning, shall have added such of the sciences as their genius shall have led them to ; the furnishing to the wealthier part of the people convenient schools at which their children may be educated at their own expense. The general objects of this law are to provide an education adapted to the years, to the capacity, and the condition of every one, and directed to their freedom and happiness. Specific details were not proper for the law. These must be the business of the visitors entrusted with its execution. The first stage of this education being the schools of the hundreds, wherein the great mass of the people will receive their instruction, the principal foundations of

future order will be laid here.   Instead, therefore, of
putting the Bible and Testament into the hands of the
children at an age when their judgments are not sufficiently matured for religious inquiries, their memories
may here be stored with the most useful facts from
Grecian, Roman, European and American history.   The
first elements of morality too may be instilled into their
minds ; such as, when further developed as their judgments advance in strength, may teach them how to work
out their own greatest happiness, by showing them that
it does not depend on the condition of life in which
chance has placed them, but is always the result of a
good conscience, good health, occupation, and freedom
in all just pursuits.   Those whom either the wealth of
their parents or the adoption of the State shall destine
to higher degrees of learning, will go on to the grammar schools, which constitute the next stage, there to
be instructed in the languages.   The learning Greek
and Latin, I am told, is going into disuse in Europe.   I
know not what their manners and occupations may call
for ; but it would be very ill-judged in us to follow
their example in this instance.   There is a certain period
of life, say from eight to fifteen or sixteen years of age,
when the mind like the body is not yet firm enough
for laborious and close operations.   If applied to such,
it falls an early victim to premature exertion ; exhibit-
ing, indeed, at first, in these young and tender subjects,
the flattering appearance of their being men while they
are yet children, but ending in reducing them to be
children when they should be men.   The memory is
then most susceptible and tenacious of impressions ;
and the learning of languages being chiefly a work of
memory, it seems precisely fitted to the powers of this
period, which is long enough too for acquiring the
most useful languages, ancient and modern.   I do not
pretend that language is science.   It is only an instrument for the attainment of science.   But that time is

not lost which is employed in providing tools for future operation ; more especially as in this case the books put into the hands of the youth for this purpose may be such as will at the same time impress their minds with useful facts and good principles. If this period be suffered to pass in idleness, the mind becomes lethargic and impotent, as would the body it inhabits if unexercised during the same time. The sympathy between body and mind during their rise, progress and decline, is too strict and obvious to endanger our being missed while we reason from the one to the other. As soon as they are of sufficient age, it is supposed they will be sent on from the grammar schools to the university, which constitutes our third and last stage, there to study those sciences which may be adapted to their views. By that part of our plan which prescribes the selection of the youths of genius from among the classes of the poor, we hope to avail the State of those talents which nature has sown as liberally among the poor as the rich, but which perish without use, if not sought for and cultivated. But of the views of this law none is more important, none more legitimate, than that of rendering the people the safe, as they are the ultimate, guardians of their own liberty. For this purpose the reading in the first stage, where *they* will receive their whole education, is proposed, as has been said, to be chiefly historical. History, by apprizing them of the past, will enable them to judge of the future ; it will avail them of the experience of other times and other nations ; it will qualify them as judges of the actions and designs of men ; it will enable them to know ambition under every disguise it may assume ; and knowing it, to defeat its views.

* * *

For this last purpose I have sketched, and put into the hands of a member a bill, delineating a practicable plan, entirely within the means they already have on hand, destined to this object. My bill proposes, 1. Elementary schools in every county, which shall place every householder within three miles of a school. 2. District colleges, which shall place every father within a day's ride of a college where he may dispose of his son. 3. An university in a healthy and central situation, with the offer of the lands, buildings, and funds of the Central College, if they will accept that place for their establishment. In the 1st will be taught reading, writing, common arithmetic, and general notions of geography. In the 2d, ancient and modern languages, geography fully, a higher degree of numerical arithmetic, mensuration, and the elementary principles of navigation. In the 3d, all the useful sciences in their highest degree. To all of which is added a selection from the elementary schools of subjects of the most promising genius, whose parents are too poor to give them further education, to be carried at the public expense through the colleges and university. The object is to bring into action that mass of talents which lies buried in poverty in every country, for want of the means of development, and thus give activity to a mass of mind, which, in proportion to our population, shall be the double or treble of what it is in most countries. The expense of the elementary schools for every county, is proposed to be levied on the wealth of the county, and all children rich and poor to be educated at these three years gratis. This is in fact and substance the plan I proposed in a bill forty years ago, but accommodated to the circumstances of this, instead of that day.

* * *

We wish to establish in the upper country, and more centrally for the State, an University on a plan so broad and liberal and *modern*, as to be worth patronizing with the public support, and be a temptation to the youth of other States to come and drink of the cup of knowledge and fraternize with us. The first step is to obtain a good plan ; that is, a judicious selection of the sciences, and a practicable grouping of some of them together, and ramifying of others, so as to adopt the professorships to our uses and our means. In an institution meant chiefly for use, some branches of science, formerly esteemed, may be now omitted ; so may others now valued in Europe, but useless to us for ages to come.

I will venture even to sketch the sciences which seem useful and practicable for us, as they occur to me while holding my pen. Botany, chemistry, zoology, anatomy, surgery, medicine, natural philosophy, agriculture, mathematics, astronomy, geography, politics, commerce, history, ethics, law, arts, fine arts. This list is imperfect because I make it hastily, and because I am unequal to the subject. We should propose to draw from Europe the first characters in science, by considerable temptations, which would not need to be repeated after the first set should have prepared fit successors and given reputation to the institution.

* * *

Our post-revolutionary youth are born under happier stars than you * and I were. They acquire all learning in their mother's womb, and bring it into the world ready made. The information of books is no longer necessary ; and all knowledge which is not innate, is in contempt, or neglect at least. Every folly must run its round ; and so, I suppose, must that of self-learning and self-sufficiency ; of rejecting the knowledge acquired in past ages, and starting on the new ground of intuition. When sobered by experience, I hope our successors will turn their attention to the advantages of education. I mean of education on the broad scale, and

* John Adams.

not that of the petty *academies*, as they call themselves, which are starting up in every neighborhood, and where one or two men, possessing Latin and sometimes Greek, a knowledge of the globes, and the first six books of Euclid, imagine and communicate this as the sum of science. They commit their pupils to the theatre of the world, with just taste enough of learning to be alienated from industrious pursuits, and not enough to do service in the ranks of science. We have some exceptions, indeed. I presented one to you lately, and we have some others. But the terms I use are general truths. I hope the necessity will, at length, be seen of establishing institutions here, as in Europe, where every branch of science, useful at this day, may be taught in its highest degree. Have you ever turned your thoughts to the plan of such an institution ? I mean to a specification of the particular sciences of real use in human affairs, and how they might be so grouped as to require so many professors only as might bring them within the views of a just but enlightened economy ?

* * *

Nobody can doubt my zeal for the general instruction of the people. Who first started that idea ? I may surely say, myself. Turn to the bill in the revised code, which I drew more than forty years ago, and before which the idea of a plan for the education of the people, generally, had never been suggested in this State. There you will see developed the first rudiments of the whole system of general education we are now urging and acting on ; and it is well known to those with whom I have acted on this subject, that I never have proposed a sacrifice of the primary to the ultimate grade of instruction. Let us keep our eye steadily on the whole system.

* * *

Of that of a professorship of the principles of government, you * express your approbation. They will be founded in the rights of man. That of agriculture, I am sure, you will approve ; and that also of Anglo-Saxon. As the histories and laws left us in that type and dialect, must be the text books of the reading of the learners, they will imbibe with the language their free principles of government.

* * *

Shall we suppress the impost and give that advantage to foreign over domestic manufactures ? On a few articles of more general and necessary use, the suppression in due season will doubtless be right, but the great mass of the articles on which impost is paid is foreign luxuries, purchased by those only who are rich enough to afford themselves the use of them. Their patriotism would certainly prefer its continuance and application to the great purposes of the public education, roads, rivers, canals, and such other objects of public improvement as it may be thought proper to add to the constitutional enumeration of federal powers. By these operations new channels of communication will be opened between the States ; the lines of separation will disappear, their interests will be identified, and their union cemented by new and indissoluble ties. Education is here placed among the articles of public care, not that it would be proposed to take its ordinary branches out of the hands of private enterprise, which manages so much better all the concerns to which it is equal ; but a public institution can alone supply those sciences which, though rarely called for, are yet necessary to complete the circle, all the parts of which contribute to the improvement of the country, and some of them to its preservation.

* Major John Cartwright.

The present consideration of a national establishment for education, particularly, is rendered proper by this circumstance also, that if Congress, approving the proposition, shall yet think it more eligible to found it on a donation of lands, they have it now in their power to endow it with those which will be among the earliest to produce the necessary income.

* * *

The probable accumulation of the surpluses of revenue beyond what can be applied to the payment of the public debt, whenever the freedom and safety of our commerce shall be restored, merits the consideration of Congress. Shall it lie unproductive in the public vaults ? Shall the revenue be reduced ? Or shall it rather be appropriated to the improvements of roads, canals, rivers, education, and other great foundations of prosperity and union, under the powers which Congress may already possess, or such amendment of the constitution as may be approved by the States ? While uncertain of the course of things, the time may be advantageously employed in obtaining the powers necessary for a system of improvement, should that be thought best.

* * *

The effect of this institution * on the future fame, fortune and prosperity of our country, can as yet be seen but at a distance. But an hundred well-educated youths, which it will turn out annually, and ere long, will fill all its offices with men of superior qualifications, and raise it from its humble state to an eminence among its associates which it has never yet known ; no, not in its brightest days. That institution is now qualified to raise its youth to an order of science unequalled

* The University of Virginia.

in any other State ; and this superiority will be the greater from the free range of mind encouraged there, and the restraint imposed at other seminaries by the shackles of a domineering hierarchy, and a bigoted adhesion to ancient habits. Those now on the theatre of affairs will enjoy the ineffable happiness of seeing themselves succeeded by sons of a grade of science beyond their own ken. Our sister States will also be repairing to the same fountains of instruction, will bring hither their genius to be kindled at our fire, and will carry back the fraternal affections which, nourished by the same *alma mater*, will knit us to them by the indissoluble bonds of early personal friendships. The good Old Dominion, the blessed mother of us all, will then raise her head with pride among the nations, will present to them that splendor of genius which she has ever possessed, but has too long suffered to rest uncultivated and unknown, and will become a centre of ralliance to the States whose youth she has instructed, and, as it were, adopted.

AMERICAN INTERNAL AFFAIRS

I. The Constitution

The absence of express declarations ensuring freedom of religion, freedom of the press, freedom of the person under the uninterrupted protection of the Habeas corpus, and trial by jury in Civil as well as in Criminal cases, excited my jealousy ; and the re-eligibility of the President for life, I quite disapproved.

* * *

How do you * like our new constitution ? I confess there are things in it which stagger all my dispositions

* John Adams.

to subscribe to what such an Assembly has proposed. The house of federal representatives will not be adequate to the management of affairs, either foreign or federal. Their President seems a bad edition of a Polish King. He may be elected from four years to four years, for life. Reason and experience prove to us, that a chief magistrate, so continuable, is an office for life. When one or two generations shall have proved that this is an office for life, it becomes, on every occasion, worthy of intrigue, of bribery, of force, and even of foreign interference. It will be of great consequence to France and England, to have America governed by a Galloman or Angloman. Once in office, and possessing the military force of the Union, without the aid or check of a council, he would not be easily dethroned, even if the people could be induced to withdraw their votes from him. I wish that at the end of the four years, they had made him forever ineligible a second time.

* * *

Virginia will insist on annexing a bill of rights to the new Constitution, i. e., a bill wherein the government shall declare that, 1. Religion shall be free ; 2. Printing presses free ; 3. Trials by jury preserved in all cases ; 4. No monopolies in commerce ; 5. No standing army.

* * *

There are two amendments only which I am anxious for : 1. A bill of rights, which it is so much the interest of all to have, that I conceive it must be yielded. The 1st amendment proposed by Massachusetts will in some degree answer this end, but not so well. It will do too much in some instances, and too little in others. It will cripple the Federal Government in some cases where it ought to be free, and not restrain in some others where restraint would be right. The 2d amendment which appears to me essential is the restoring the principle of necessary rotation, particularly to the Senate and Presidency : but most of all to the last. Re-eligibility makes him an officer for life, and the disasters inseparable from an elective monarchy, render it preferable if we cannot tread back that step, that we should go forward and take refuge in an hereditary one. Of the correction of this article, however, I entertain no present hope, because I find it has scarcely excited an objection in America. And if it does not take place ere-long, it assuredly never will. The natural progress of things is for liberty to yield and government to gain ground. As yet our spirits are free. Our jealousy is only put to sleep by the unlimited confidence we all repose in the person to whom we all look as our president. After him inferior characters may perhaps succeed, and awaken us to the danger which his merit has led us into.

* * *

I congratulate you * on the accession of your State to the new federal constitution. This is the last I have yet heard of, but I expect daily to hear that my own has followed the good example, and suppose it to be already established. Our government wanted bracing. Still, we must take care not to run from one extreme to another ; not to brace too high. I own, I join those in opinion, who think a bill of rights necessary. I apprehend too, that the total abandonment of the principle of rotation in the offices of President and Senator, will end in abuse. But my confidence is, that there will, for a long time, be virtue and good sense enough in our countrymen, to correct abuses. We can surely boast of having set the world a beautiful example of a government reformed by reason alone, without bloodshed. But the world is too far oppressed, to profit by

* Edward Rutledge.

the example. On this side of the Atlantic, the blood
of the people is become an inheritance, and those who
fatten on it, will not relinquish it easily.

* * *

You * say that I have been dished up to you as an
anti-federalist, and ask me if it be just. I am not a fed-
eralist, because I never submitted the whole system of
my opinions to the creed of any party of men whatever,
in religion, in philosophy, in politics or in anything
else, where I was capable of thinking for myself. Such
an addiction, is the last degradation of a free and moral
agent. If I could not go to heaven but with a party,
I would not go there at all. Therefore, I am not of the
party of federalists. But I am much farther from that
of the anti-federalists. I approved, from the first moment, of the great mass of what is in the new Constitution ; the consolidation of the government ; the organization into executive, legislative, and judiciary ; the
subdivision of the legislative ; the happy compromise of
interests between the great and little States, by the different manner of voting in the different Houses ; the
voting by persons instead of States ; the qualified nega-
tive on laws given to the executive, which, however, I
should have liked better if associated with the judiciary
also, as in New York ; and the power of taxation. I
thought at first that the latter might have been limited.
A little reflection soon convinced me it ought not to be.
What I disapproved from the first moment also, was
the want of a bill of rights, to guard liberty against the
legislative as well as the executive branches of the
government ; that is to say, to secure freedom in religion, freedom of the press, freedom from monopolies,
freedom from unlawful imprisonment, freedom from a
permanent military, and a trial by jury, in all cases

* F. Hopkinson.

determinable by the laws of the land. I disapproved, also, the perpetual re-eligibility of the President. To these points of disapprobation I adhere.

With respect to the declaration of rights, I suppose the majority of the United States are of my opinion ; for I apprehend, all the anti-federalists and a very respectable proportion of the federalists, think that such a declaration should now be annexed. The enlightened part of Europe have given us the greatest credit for inventing the instrument of security for the rights of the people, and have been not a little surprised to see us so soon give it up. With respect to the re-eligibility of the President, I find myself differing from the majority of my countrymen ; for I think there are but three States out of the eleven which have desired an alteration of this. And indeed, since the thing is established, I would wish it not to be altered during the life of our great leader, whose executive talents are superior to those, I believe, of any man in the world, and who, alone, by the authority of his name and the confidence reposed in his perfect integrity, is fully qualified to put the new government so under way, as to secure it against the efforts of opposition. But, having derived from our error all the good there was in it, I hope we shall correct it, the moment we can no longer have the same name at the helm.

* * *

I cannot refrain from making short answers to the objections which your * letter states to have been raised. Experience proves the inefficacy of a bill of rights. True. But though it is not absolutely efficacious under all circumstances, it is of great potency always, and rarely inefficacious. A brace the more will often keep up the building which would have fallen, with that brace the less. There is a remarkable difference between the

* James Madison.

characters of the inconveniences which attend a declaration of rights, and those which attend the want of it. The inconveniences of the declaration are, that it may cramp government in its useful exertions. But the evil of this is short-lived, moderate and reparable. The inconveniences of the want of a declaration are permanent, afflicting and irreparable. They are in constant progression from bad to worse. The executive, in our governments, is not the sole, it is scarcely the principal object of my jealousy. The tyranny of the legislatures is the most formidable dread at present, and will be for many years. That of the executive will come in its turn ; but it will be at a remote period.

* * *

There are rights which it is useless to surrender to the government, and which governments have yet always been found to invade. These are the rights of thinking, and publishing our thoughts by speaking or writing ; the right of free commerce ; the right of personal freedom. There are instruments for administering the government, so peculiarly trust-worthy, that we should never leave the legislature at liberty to change them.

* * *

On similar ground it may be proved, that no society can make a perpetual constitution, or even a perpetual law. The earth belongs always to the living generation : they may manage it, then, and what proceeds from it, as they please, during their usufruct. They are masters, too, of their own persons, and consequently may govern them as they please. But persons and property make the sum of the objects of government. The constitution and the laws of their predecessors are extinguished then, in their natural course, with those whose will gave them being. This could preserve that being, till it ceased to be itself, and no longer. Every constitution, then, and every law, naturally expires at the end of thirty-four years.

* * *

Some men look at constitutions with sanctimonious reverence, and deem them like the ark of the covenant, too sacred to be touched. They ascribe to the men of the preceding age a wisdom more than human, and suppose what they did to be beyond amendment. I knew that age well ; I belonged to it, and labored with it. It deserved well of its country. It was very like the present, but without the experience of the present ; and forty years of experience in government is worth a century of book-reading ; and this they would say themselves, were they to rise from the dead. I am certainly not an advocate for frequent and untried changes in laws and constitutions. I think moderate imperfections had better be borne with ; because, when once known, we accommodate ourselves to them, and find practical means of correcting their ill effects. But I know also, that laws and institutions must go hand in hand with the progress of the human mind. As that becomes more developed, more enlightened, as new discoveries are made, new truths disclosed, and manners and opinions change with the change of circumstances, institutions must advance also, and keep pace with the times. We might as well require a man to wear still the coat which fitted him when a boy, as civilized society to remain ever under the regimen of their barbarous ancestors. Therefore, let us provide in our constitution for its revision at stated periods. What these periods should be, nature herself indicates. By the European tables of mortality, of the adults living at any one moment of time, a majority will be dead in about nineteen years. At the end of that period then, a new majority is come into place ; or, in other words, a new generation. Each generation is as independent of the one preceding, as that was of all which had gone before. It has then, like them, a right to choose for itself the form of government it believes most promotive of its own happiness ; consequently, to accommodate to the circumstances in which it finds itself, that received from its predecessors ; and it is for the peace and good of mankind, that a solemn opportunity of doing this every nineteen or twenty years, should be provided by the constitution ; so that it may be handed on, with periodical repairs, from generation to generation, to the end of time, if anything human can so long endure. If this avenue be shut to the call of sufferance, it will make itself heard through that of force, and we shall go on, as other nations are doing, in the endless circle of oppression, rebellion, reformation ; and oppression, rebellion, reformation, again ; and so on forever.

* * *

But, whatever be the constitution, great care must be taken to provide a mode of amendment, when experience or change of circumstances shall have manifested that any part of it is unadapted to the good of the nation. In some of our States it requires a new authority from the whole people, acting by their representatives, chosen for this express purpose, and assembled in convention. This is found too difficult for remedying the imperfections which experience develops from time to time in an organization of the first impression. A greater facility of amendment is certainly requisite to maintain it in a course of action accommodated to the times and changes through which we are ever passing.

* * *

The term *constitution* in jurisprudence, whenever it is applied to any act of the legislature, invariably means a statute, law, or ordinance. To get rid of the magic supposed to be in the word *constitution*, let us translate it into its definition as given by those who think it above the power of the law ; and let us suppose the convention, instead of saying, "We the ordinary legislature, establish a *constitution*," had said, "We the ordinary legislature, establish an act *above the power of the ordinary legislature*." Does not this expose the absurdity of the attempt ?

* * *

I told him,* that in my opinion, there was only a single source of these discontents. Though they had indeed appeared to spread themselves over the War department also, yet I considered that as an overflowing only from their real channel, which would never have taken place, if they had not first been generated in another department, to wit, that of the Treasury. That a system had there been contrived, for deluging the States with paper money instead of gold and silver, for withdrawing our citizens from the pursuits of commerce, manufactures, buildings, and other branches of useful industry, to occupy themselves and their capitals in a species of gambling, destructive of morality, and which had introduced its poison into the government itself. That it was a fact, as certainly known as that he and I were then conversing, that particular members of the legislature, while those laws were on the carpet, had feathered their nests with paper, had then voted for the laws, and constantly since lent all the energy of their talents, and instrumentality of their offices, to the establishment and enlargement of this system ; that they had chained it about our necks for a great length of time, and in order to keep the game in their hands had, from time to time, aided in making such legislative constructions of the constitution, as made it a very different

* President Washington.

thing from what the people thought they had submitted to ; that they had now brought forward a proposition far beyond any one ever yet advanced, and to which the eyes of many were turned, as the decision which was to let us know, whether we live under a limited or an unlimited government.

II. THE JUDICIARY

It is not enough that honest men are appointed Judges. All know the influence of interest on the mind of man, and how unconsciously his judgment is warped by that influence. To this bias add that of the *esprit de corps,* of their peculiar maxim and creed, that "it is the office of a good Judge to enlarge his jurisdiction," and the absence of responsibility ; and how can we expect impartial decision between the General government, of which they are themselves so eminent a part, and an individual State, from which they have nothing to hope or fear ? We have seen, too, that contrary to all correct example, they are in the habit of going out of the question before them, to throw an anchor ahead, and grapple further hold for future advances of power. They are then, in fact, the corps of sappers and miners, steadily working to undermine the independent rights of the States, and to consolidate all power in the hands of that government in which they have so important a freehold estate.

* * *

The opinion which gives to the judges the right to decide what laws are constitutional, and what not, not only for themselves in their own sphere of action, but for the Legislature and executive also, in their spheres, would make the judiciary a despotic branch.

* * *

The death of Cushing is opportune, as it gives an opening for at length getting a republican majority on the supreme bench. Ten years has the anti-civism of that body been bidding defiance to the spirit of the whole nation, after they had manifested their will by reforming every other branch of the government. I trust the occasion will not be lost.

* * *

The event is a fortunate one, and so timed as to be a God-send to me. I am sure its importance to the nation will be felt, and the occasion employed to complete the great operation they have so long been executing, by the appointment of a decided republican, with nothing equivocal about him.

* * *

The question, whether the judges are invested with exclusive authority to decide on the constitutionality of a law, has been heretofore a subject of consideration with me in the exercise of official duties. Certainly there is not a word in the constitution which has given that power to them more than to the executive or legislative branches. Questions of property, of character and of crime being ascribed to the judges, through a definite course of legal proceeding, laws involving such questions belong, of course, to them ; and as they decide on them ultimately and without appeal, they of course decide *for themselves*. The constitutional validity of the law or laws again prescribing executive action, and to be administered by that branch ultimately and without appeal, the executive must decide for *themselves* also, whether, under the constitution, they are valid or not. So also as to laws governing the proceedings of the legislature, that body must judge *for itself* the constitutionality of the law, and equally without appeal or control from its co-ordinate branches. And, in general, that branch which is to act ultimately, and without appeal, on any law, is the rightful expositor of the validity of the law, uncontrolled by the opinions of the other co-ordinate authorities. It may be said that contradictory decisions may arise in such case, and produce inconvenience. This is possible, and is a necessary failing in all human proceedings. But there is another opinion entertained by some men of such judgment and information as to lessen my confidence in my own. That is, that the legislature alone is the exclusive expounder of the sense of the constitution, in every part of it whatever. And they allege in its support, that this branch has authority to impeach and punish a member of either of the others acting contrary to its declaration of the sense of the constitution. It may indeed be answered, that an act may still be valid although the party is punished for it, right or wrong. However, this opinion which ascribes exclusive exposition to the legislature, merits respect for its safety, there being in the body of the nation a control over them, which, if expressed by rejection on the subsequent exercise of their elective franchise, enlists public opinion against their exposition, and encourages a judge or executive on a future occasion to adhere to their former opinion. Between these two doctrines, every one has a right to choose, and I know of no third meriting any respect.

In denying the right they * usurp of exclusively explaining the constitution, I go further than you † do. For, intending to establish three departments, co-ordinate and independent, that they might check and balance one another, it (the constitution) has given, according to this opinion, to one of them alone, the right to prescribe rules for the government of the others, and to

* The judiciary.
† Thomas Leiper.

that one too, which is unelected by, and independent
of the nation.

*   *   *

The constitution, on this hypothesis, is a mere thing
of wax in the hands of the judiciary, which they may
twist and shape into any form they please. It should
be remembered, as an axiom of eternal truth in politics, that whatever power in any government is independent, is absolute also ; in theory only, at first, while
the spirit of the people is up, but in practice, as fast as
that relaxes. Independence can be trusted nowhere
but with the people in mass. They are inherently independent of all but moral law.

*   *   *

You * seem to consider the judges as the ultimate
arbiters of all constitutional questions ; a very dangerous
doctrine indeed, and one which would place us under
the despotism of an oligarchy. Our judges are as honest
as other men, and not more so. They have, with others, the same passions for party, for power, and the
privilege of their corps. Their maxim is "*boni judicis
est ampliare jurisdictionem,*" and their power the more
dangerous as they are in office for life, and not responsible, as the other functionaries are, to the elective
control. The constitution has erected no such single
tribunal, knowing that to whatever hands confided, with
the corruptions of time and party, its members would
become despots. It has more wisely made all the departments co-equal and co-sovereign within themselves.

*   *   *

The germ of dissolution of our federal government is
in the constitution of the federal judiciary ; an irre-
* Mr. Jarvis.

sponsible body, (for impeachment is scarcely a scare-
crow,) working like gravity by night and by day, gain-
ing a little to-day and a little to-morrow, and advancing its noiseless step like a thief, over the field of jurisdiction, until all shall be usurped from the States, and
the government of all be consolidated into one. To
this I am opposed ; because, when all government, domestic and foreign, in little as in great things, shall be
drawn to Washington as the centre of all power, it
will render powerless the checks provided of one government on another, and will become as venal and oppressive as the government from which we separated.
It will be as in Europe, where every man must be either
pike or gudgeon, hammer or anvil. Our functionaries
and theirs are wares from the same work-shop ; made
of the same materials, and by the same hand. If the
States look with apathy on this silent descent of their
government into the gulf which is to swallow all, we
have only to weep over the human character formed un-
controlable but by a rod of iron, and the blasphemers
of man, as incapable of self-government; become his true
historians.

* * *

I cannot lay down my pen without recurring to one
of the subjects of my former letter, for in truth there
is no danger I apprehend so much as the consolidation
of our government by the noiseless, and therefore un-
alarming, instrumentality of the supreme court. This
is the form in which federalism now arrays itself, and
consolidation is the present principle of distinction between republicans and the pseudo-republicans but real
federalists.

* * *

This practice of Judge Marshall, of travelling out of
his case to prescribe what the law would be in a moot

case not before the court, is very irregular and very censurable.

* * *

At the establishment of our constitutions, the judiciary bodies were supposed to be the most helpless and harmless members of the government. Experience, however, soon showed in what way they were to become the most dangerous ; that the insufficiency of the means provided for their removal gave them a freehold and irresponsibility in office ; that their decisions, seeming to concern individual suitors only, pass silent and unheeded by the public at large ; that these decisions, nevertheless, become law by precedent, sapping, by little and little, the foundations of the constitution, and working its change by construction, before any one has perceived that that invisible and helpless worm has been busily employed in consuming its substance. In truth, man is not made to be trusted for life, if secured against all liability to account.

* * *

One single object, if your provision attains it, will entitle you * to the endless gratitude of society ; that of restraining judges from usurping legislation.   And with no body of men is this restraint more wanting than with the judges of what is commonly called our general government, but what I call our foreign department. They are practising on the constitution by inferences, analogies, and sophisms, as they would on an ordinary law.   They do not seem aware that it is not even a *constitution*, formed by a single authority, and subject to a single superintendence and control ; but that it is a compact of many independent powers, every single one of which claims an equal right to understand it, and to require its observance.

* Edward Livingston.

III. FINANCE AND DEBT

Among many good qualities which my countrymen possess, some of a different character unhappily mix themselves. The most remarkable are, indolence, extravagance, and infidelity to their engagements. Cure the two first, and the last would disappear, because it is a consequence of them, and not proceeding from a want of morals. I know of no remedy against indolence and extravagance, but a free course of justice. Everything else is merely palliative ; but unhappily, the evil has gained too generally the mass of the nation, to leave the course of justice unobstructed. The maxim of buying nothing without the money in our pockets to pay for it, would make of our country one of the happiest upon earth. Experience during the war proved this ; as I think every man will remember, that under all the privations it obliged him to submit to, during that period, he slept sounder, and awaked happier than he can do now. Desperate of finding relief from a free course of justice, I look forward to the abolition of all credit, as the only other remedy which can take place.

* * *

The question, whether one generation of men has a right to bind another, seems never to have been started either on this or our side of the water. Yet it is a question of such consequences as not only to merit decision, but place also among the fundamental principles of every government. The course of reflection in which we are immersed here, on the elementary principles of society, has presented this question to my mind ; and that no such obligation can be transmitted, I think very capable of proof. I set out on this ground, which I suppose to be self-evident, that the *earth belongs in usufruct to the living* ; that the dead have neither powers nor rights over it.   The portion occupied by any individual ceases to be his when himself ceases to be, and reverts to the society.   If the society has formed no rules for the appropriation of its lands in severalty, it will be taken by the first occupants, and these will generally be the wife and children of the decedent.   If they have formed rules of appropriation, those rules may give it to the wife and children, or to some one of them, or to the legatee of the deceased.   So they may give it to its creditor. But the child, the legatee or creditor, takes it, not by natural right, but by a law of the society of which he is a member, and to which he is subject.   Then, no man can, by *natural right*, oblige the lands he occupied, or the persons who succeed him in that occupation, to the payment of debts contracted by him.   Then I say, the earth belongs to each of these generations during its course, fully and in its own right.   The second generation receives it clear of the debts and incumbrances of the first, the third of the second, and so on.   For if the first could charge it with a debt, then the earth would belong to the dead and not to the living generation.   Then, no generation can contract debts greater than may be paid during the course of its own existence.

* * *

I wish it were possible to obtain a single amendment to our Constitution.   I would be willing to depend on that alone for the reduction of the administration of our government to the genuine principles of its Constitution ; I mean an additional article, taking from the federal government the power of borrowing.

* * *

I consider the fortunes of our republic as depending, in an eminent degree, on the extinguishment of the public debt before we engage in any war : because, that done, we shall have revenue enough to improve our country in peace and defend it in war, without recurring either to new taxes or loans. But if the debt should once more be swelled to a formidable size, its entire discharge will be despaired of, and we shall be committed to the English career of debt, corruption and rottenness, closing with revolution. The discharge of the debt, therefore, is vital to the destinies of our government.

* * *

We are all the more reconciled to the tax on importations, because it falls exclusively on the rich, and with the equal partition of intestate's estates, constitute the best agrarian law. In fact, the poor man in this country who uses nothing but what is made within his own farm or family, or within the United States, pays not a farthing of tax to the general government, but on his salt ; and should we go into that manufacture as we ought to do, we will pay not one cent. Our revenues once liberated by the discharge of the public debt, and its surplus applied to canals, roads, schools, &c., and the farmer will see his government supported, his children educated, and the face of his country made a paradise by the contributions of the rich alone, without his being called on to spare a cent from his earnings. The path we are now pursuing leads directly to this end, which we cannot fail to attain unless our administration should fall into unwise hands.

* * *

It is a wise rule, and should be fundamental in a government disposed to cherish its credit, and at the same time to restrain the use of it within the limits of its faculties, "never to borrow a dollar without laying a tax in the same instant for paying the interest annually, and the principle within a given term ; and to consider that tax as pledged to the creditors on the public faith."

On such a pledge as this, sacredly observed, a government may always command, on a *reasonable interest*, all the lendable money of their citizens, while the necessity of an equivalent tax is a salutary warning to them and their constituents against oppressions, bankruptcy, and its inevitable consequence, revolution. But the term of redemption must be moderate, and at any rate within the limits of their rightful powers. But what limits, it will be asked, does this prescribe to their powers ? What is to hinder them from creating a perpetual debt ? The laws of nature, I answer. The earth belongs to the living, not to the dead.

* * *

At this moment, a new majority have come into place, in their own right, and not under the rights, the conditions, or laws of their predecessors. Are they bound to acknowledge the debt, to consider the preceding generation as having had a right to eat up the whole soil of their country, in the course of a life, to alienate it from them, (for it would be an alienation to the creditors,) and would they think themselves either legally or morally bound to give up their country and emigrate to another for subsistence ? Every one will say no ; that the soil is the gift of God to the living, as much as it had been to the deceased generation ; and that the laws of nature impose no obligation on them to pay this debt. And although, like some other natural rights, this has not yet entered into any declaration of rights, it is no less a law, and ought to be acted on by honest governments. It is, at the same time, a salutary curb on the spirit of war and indebtment, which, since the modern theory of the perpetuation of debt, has drenched the earth with blood, and crushed its inhabitants under burthens ever accumulating.

The earth is given as a common stock for man to live and labor on. If for the encouragement of industry, we allow the earth to be appropriated, we must take care that other employment be provided to those excluded from the appropriation. If we do not, the fundamental right to labor the earth returns.

* * *

Everything predicted by the enemies of banks, in the beginning, is now coming to pass. We are to be ruined now by the deluge of bank paper, as we were formerly by the old Continental paper. It is cruel that such revolutions in private fortunes should be at the mercy of avaricious adventurers, who, instead of employing their capital, if any they have, in manufactures, commerce, and other useful pursuits, make it an instrument to burthen all the interchanges of property with their swindling profits, profits which are the price of no useful industry of theirs.

* * *

For it never was, and is not, any confidence in their frothy bubbles, but the want of all other medium, which induced, or now induces, the *country* people to take their paper ; and at this moment, when nothing else is to be had, no man will receive it but to pass it away instantly, none for distant purposes. We are now without any common measure of the value of property, and private fortunes are up or down at the will of the worst of our citizens.

* * *

Like a dropsical man calling out for water, water, our deluded citizens are clamoring for more banks, more banks. The American mind is now in that state of fever which the world has so often seen in the history of other nations. We are under the bank bubble, as England was under the South Sea bubble, France under the Mississippi bubble, and as every nation is liable to be, under whatever bubble, design, or delusion may puff up in moments when off their guard. We are now taught to believe that legerdemain tricks upon paper can produce as solid wealth as hard labor in the earth. It is vain for common sense to urge that *nothing* can produce but *nothing* ; that it is an idle dream to believe in a philosopher's stone which is to turn everything into gold, and to redeem man from the original sentence of his Maker, "in the sweat of his brow shall he eat his bread."

* * *

The taxes with which we are familiar, class themselves readily according to the basis on which they rest. 1. Capital. 2. Income. 3. Consumption. These may be considered as commensurate ; Consumption being generally equal to Income, and Income the annual profit of Capital. A government may select either of these bases for the establishment of its system of taxation, and so frame it as to reach the faculties of every member of the society, and to draw from him his equal proportion of the public contributions ; and, if this be correctly obtained, it is the perfection of the function of taxation. But when once a government has assumed its basis, to select and tax special articles from either of the other classes, is double taxation.

To this a single observation shall yet be added. Whether property alone, and the whole of what each citizen possesses, shall be subject to contribution, or only its surplus after satisfying his first wants, or whether the faculties of body and mind shall contribute also from their annual earnings, is a question to be decided. But, when decided, and the principle settled, it is to be equally and fairly applied to all. To take from one, because it is thought that his own industry and that of his fathers has acquired too much, in order to spare to others, who, or whose fathers have not exercised equal industry and skill, is to violate arbitrarily the first principle of association, "the *guarantee* to every one of a free exercise of his industry, and the fruits acquired by it." If the overgrown wealth of an individual be deemed dangerous to the State, the best corrective is the law of equal inheritance to all in equal degree ; and the better, as this enforces a law of nature, while extra-taxation violates it.

* * *

There is, indeed, one evil which awakens me at times, because it jostles me at every turn. It is that we have now no measure of value. I am asked eighteen dollars for a yard of broadcloth, which, when we had dollars, I used to get for eighteen shillings ; from this I can only understand that a dollar is now worth but two inches of broadcloth, but broadcloth is no standard of measure or value. I do not know, therefore, whereabouts I stand in the scale of property, nor what to ask, or what to give for it. I saw, indeed, the like machinery in action in the years '80 and '81, and without dissatisfaction ; because in wearing out, it was working out our salvation. But I see nothing in this renewal of the game of "Robin's alive" but a general demoralization of the nation, a filching from industry its honest earnings, wherewith to build up palaces, and raise gambling stock for swindlers and shavers, who are to close too their career of piracies by fraudulent bankruptcies.

IV. Secession

The division of sentiment and interest happens unfortunately to be so geographical, that no mortal can say that what is most wise and temperate would prevail against what is most easy and obvious ? I can scarcely contemplate a more incalculable evil than the breaking of the Union into two or more parts. Yet when

we consider the mass which opposed the original co-
alescence ; when we consider that it lay chiefly in the
Southern quarter ; that the Legislature have availed
themselves of no occasion of allaying it, but on the
contrary, whenever Northern and Southern prejudices
have come into conflict, the latter have been sacrificed
and the former soothed ; that the owers of the debt are
in the Southern, and the holders of it in the Northern
division ; that the anti-federal champions are now
strengthened in argument by the fulfillment of their
predictions ; that this has been brought about by the
monarchical federalists themselves, who, having been
for the new government merely as a stepping stone
to monarchy, have themselves adopted the very constructions of the Constitution, of which, when advocat-
ing its acceptance before the tribunal of the people,
they declared it unsusceptible ; that the republican federalists who espoused the same government for its in-
trinsic merits, are disarmed of their weapons ; that
which they denied as prophecy, having now become
true history, who can be sure that these things may not
proselyte the small number which was wanting to place
the majority on the other side ?

* * *

After plunging us in all the broils of the European nations, there would remain but one act to close our
tragedy, that is, to break up our Union ; and even this
they have ventured seriously and solemnly to propose
and maintain by arguments in a Connecticut paper.   I
have been happy, however, in believing, from the stifling
of this effort, that that dose was found too strong, and
excited as much repugnance there as it did horror in
other parts of our country, and that whatever follies we
may be led into as to foreign nations, we shall never give
up our Union, the last anchor of our hope, and that
alone which is to prevent this heavenly country from

becoming an arena of gladiators. Much as I abhor war, and view it as the greatest scourge of mankind, and anxiously as I wish to keep out of the broils of Europe, I would yet go with my brethren into these, rather than separate from them.

* * *

But if on a temporary superiority of the one party, the other is to resort to a scission of the Union, no federal government can ever exist. If to rid ourselves of the present rule of Massachusetts and Connecticut, we break the Union, will the evil stop there ? Suppose the New England States alone cut off, will our nature be changed ? Are we not men still to the south of that, and with all the passions of men ? Immediately, we shall see a Pennsylvania and a Virginia party arise in the residuary confederacy, and the public mind will be distracted with the same party spirit. What a game too will the one party have in their hands, by eternally threatening the other that unless they do so and so, they will join their northern neighbors. If we reduce our Union to Virginia and North Carolina, immediately the conflict will be established between the representatives of these two States, and they will end by breaking into their simple units.

* * *

Dangers of another kind might more reasonably be apprehended from this perfect and distinct organization, civil and military, of the States ; to wit, that certain States from local and occasional discontents, might attempt to secede from the Union. This is certainly possible ; and would be befriended by this regular organization. But it is not probable that local discontents can spread to such an extent, as to be able to face the sound parts of so extensive an Union ; and if ever they should reach the majority, they would then become the regular government, acquire the ascendency in Congress, and be able to redress their own grievances by laws peaceably and constitutionally passed.

* * *

The Missouri question aroused and filled me with alarm. The old schism of federal and republican threatened nothing, because it existed in every State, and united them together by the fraternism of party. But the coincidence of a marked principle, moral and political, with a geographical line, once conceived, I feared would never more be obliterated from the mind ; that it would be recurring on every occasion and renewing irritations, until it would kindle such mutual and mortal hatred, as to render separation preferable to eternal discord. I have been among the most sanguine in believing that our Union would be of long duration. I now doubt it much, and see the event at no great distance, and the direct consequence of this question ; not by the line which has been so confidently counted on ; the laws of nature control this ; but by the Potomac, Ohio and Missouri, or more probably, the Mississippi upwards to our northern boundary.

* * *

Whilst the General Assembly thus declares the rights retained by the States, rights which they have never yielded, and which this State will never voluntarily yield, they do not mean to raise the banner of disaffection, or of separation from their sister States, co-parties with themselves to this compact. They know and value too highly the blessings of their Union as to foreign nations and questions arising among themselves, to consider every infraction as to be met by actual resistance. They respect too affectionately the opinions of those possessing the same rights under the same instrument, to make every difference of construction a ground of immediate rupture. They would, indeed, consider such a rupture as among the greatest calamities which could befall them ; but not the greatest. There is yet one greater, submission to a government of unlimited powers. In the meanwhile, we will breast with them, rather than separate from them, every misfortune, save that only of living under a government of unlimited powers. We owe every other sacrifice to ourselves, to our federal brethren, and to the world at large, to pursue with temper and perseverance the great experiment which shall prove that man is capable of living in society, governing itself by laws self-imposed, and securing to its members the enjoyment of life, liberty, property, and peace ; and further to show, that even when the government of its choice shall manifest a tendency to degeneracy, we are not at once to despair but that the will and the watchfulness of its sounder parts will reform its aberrations, recall it to original and legitimate principles, and restrain it within the rightful limits of self-government.

* * *

V. SLAVERY

There must doubtless be an unhappy influence on the manners of our people produced by the existence of slavery among us. The whole commerce between master and slave is a perpetual exercise of the most boisterous passions, the most unremitting despotism on the one part, and degrading submissions on the other. Our children see this, and learn to imitate it ; for man is an imitative animal. This quality is the germ of all education in him. From his cradle to his grave he is learning to do what he sees others do. If a parent could find no motive either in his philanthropy or his self-love, for restraining the intemperance of passion towards his slave, it should always be a sufficient one that his child is present.   But generally it is not sufficient.   The parent storms, the child looks on, catches the lineaments of wrath, puts on the same airs in the circle of smaller slaves, gives a loose to the worst of passions, and thus nursed, educated, and daily exercised in tyranny, cannot but be stamped by it with odious peculiarities.   The man must be a prodigy who can retain his manners and morals undepraved by such circumstances.   And with what execration should the statesman be loaded, who, permitting one half the citizens thus to trample on the rights of the other, transforms those into despots, and these into enemies, destroys the morals of the one part, and the *amor patriæ* of the other.   For if a slave can have a country in this world, it must be any other in preference to that in which he is born to live and labor for another ; in which he must lock up the faculties of his nature, contribute as far as depends on his individual endeavors to the evanishment of the human race, or entail his own miserable condition on the endless generations proceeding from him.   With the morals of the people, their industry also is destroyed.   For in a warm climate, no man will labor for himself who can make another labor for him.   This is so true, that of the proprietors of slaves a very small proportion indeed are ever seen to labor.   And can the liberties of a nation be thought secure when we have removed their only firm basis, a conviction in the minds of the people that these liberties are of the gift of God ?   That they are not to be violated but with his wrath ?   Indeed I tremble for my country when I reflect that God is just ; that his justice cannot sleep forever ; that considering numbers, nature and natural means only, a revolution of the wheel of fortune, an exchange of situation is among possible events ; that it may become probable by supernatural interference !   The Almighty has no attribute which can take side with us in such a contest.   But it is impossible to be temperate and to pursue this subject through the various considerations of policy, of morals, of history natural and civil.

* * *

The clause, too, reprobating the enslaving the inhabitants of Africa, was struck out in complaisance to South Carolina and Georgia, who had never attempted to restrain the importation of slaves, and who, on the contrary, still wished to continue it. Our northern brethren also, I believe, felt a little tender under those censures ; for although their people had very few slaves themselves, yet they had been pretty considerable carriers of them to others.

* * *

South Carolina and Georgia, therefore, struck up a bargain with the three New England States. If they would join to admit slaves for some years, the southernmost States would join in changing the clause which required two-thirds of the legislature in any vote. It was done.

* * *

As to the mode of emancipation, I am satisfied that that must be a matter of compromise between the passions, the prejudices, and the real difficulties which will each have their weight in that operation. Perhaps the first chapter of this history, which has begun in St. Domingo, and the next succeeding ones, which will recount how all the whites were driven from all the other islands, may prepare our minds for a peaceable accommodation between justice, policy and necessity ; and furnish an answer to the difficult question, whither shall the colored emigrants go ? and the sooner we put some plan under way, the greater hope there is that it may be permitted to proceed peaceably to its ultimate effect.   But if something is not done, and soon done, we shall be the murderers of our own children.   The "murmura venturos nautis prudentia ventos" has already reached us ; the revolutionary storm, now sweeping the globe, will be upon us, and happy if we make timely provision to give it an easy passage over our land.   From the present state of things in Europe and America, the day which begins our combustion must be near at hand ; and only a single spark is wanting to make that day to-morrow.   If we had begun sooner, we might probably have been allowed a lengthier operation to clear our-selves, but every day's delay lessens the time we may take for emancipation.

*   *   *

I concur entirely in your leading principles of gradual emancipation, of establishment on the coast of Africa, and the patronage of our nation until the emigrants shall be able to protect themselves.   The subordinate details might be easily arranged.   But the bare proposition of purchase by the United States generally, would excite infinite indignation in all the States north of Maryland. The sacrifice must fall on the States alone which hold them ; and the difficult question will be how to lessen this so as to reconcile our fellow citizens to it.   Per-sonally I am ready and desirous to make any sacrifice which shall ensure their gradual but complete retire-ment from the State, and effectually, at the same time, establish them elsewhere in freedom and safety.   But I have not perceived the growth of this disposition in the rising generation, of which I once had sanguine hopes. No symptoms inform me that it will take place in my day.   I leave it, therefore, to time, and not at all with-out hope that the day will come, equally desirable and welcome to us as to them. Perhaps the proposition now on the carpet at Washington to provide an establishment on the coast of Africa for voluntary emigrations of people of color, may be the corner stone of this future edifice.

* * *

With us things are going on well. The boisterous sea of liberty indeed is never without a wave, and that from Missouri is now rolling towards us, but we shall ride over it as we have over all others. It is not a moral question, but one merely of power. Its object is to raise a geographical principle for the choice of a president, and the noise will be kept up till that is effected. All know that permitting the slaves of the south to spread into the west will not add one being to that unfortunate condition, that it will increase the happiness of those existing, and by spreading them over a larger surface, will dilute the evil everywhere, and facilitate the means of getting finally rid of it, an event more anxiously wished by those on whom it presses than by the noisy pretenders to exclusive humanity. In the meantime, it is a ladder for rivals climbing to power.

Our only blot is becoming less offensive by the great improvement in the condition and civilization of that race, who can now more advantageously compare their situation with that of the laborers of Europe. Still it is a hideous blot, as well from the heteromorph peculiarities of the race, as that, with them, physical compulsion to action must be substituted for the moral necessity which constrains the free laborers to work equally hard. We feel and deplore it morally and politically, and we look without entire despair to some redeeming means not yet specifically foreseen. I am happy in believing that the conviction of the necessity of removing this evil gains ground with time. Their emigration to the

westward lightens the difficulty by dividing it, and
renders it more practicable on the whole.

* * *

I congratulate you, fellow citizens, on the approach
of the period at which you may interpose your authority
constitutionally, to withdraw the citizens of the United
States from all further participation in those violations
of human rights which have been so long continued on
the unoffending inhabitants of Africa, and which the
morality, the reputation, and the best interests of our
country, have long been eager to proscribe. Although
no law you may pass can take prohibitory effect till the
first day of the year one thousand eight hundred and
eight, yet the intervening period is not too long to prevent, by timely notice, expeditions which cannot be
completed before that day.

FOREIGN RELATIONS, WAR AND PEACE

War between two nations cannot diminish the rights
of the rest of the world remaining at peace. The doctrine that the rights of nations remaining quietly in the
exercise of moral and social duties, are to give way to the
convenience of those who prefer plundering and mur-
dering one another, is a monstrous doctrine ; and ought
to yield to the more rational law, that "the wrong which
two nations endeavor to inflict on each other, must not
infringe on the rights or conveniences of those remaining at peace." And what is *contraband*, by the law of
nature ? Either everything which may aid or comfort
an enemy, or nothing. Either all commerce which
would accommodate him is unlawful, or none is. The
difference between articles of one or another description, is a difference in degree only. No line between
them can be drawn. Either all intercourse must cease
between neutrals and belligerents, or all be permitted.

Can the world hesitate to say which shall be the rule ?
Shall two nations turning tigers, break up in one instant
the peaceable relations of the whole world ?   Reason
and nature clearly pronounce that the neutral is to go
on in the enjoyment of all its rights, that its commerce
remains free, not subject to the jurisdiction of another,
nor consequently its vessels to search, or to enquiries
whether their contents are the property of an enemy, or
are of those which have been called contraband of war.

* * *

I think, therefore, that while we do nothing which the
first nation on earth would deem crouching, we had
better give to all our communications with them a very
mild, complaisant, and even friendly complexion, but
always independent.   Ask no favors, leave small and
irritating things to be conducted by the individuals interested in them, interfere ourselves but in the greatest
cases, and then not push them to irritation.   No matter
at present existing between them and us is important
enough to risk a breach of peace ; peace being indeed
the most important of all things for us, except the preserving an erect and independent attitude.

* * *

What, in short, is the whole system of Europe towards
America but an atrocious and insulting tyranny ?   One
hemisphere of the earth, separated from the other by
wide seas on both sides, having a different system of
interests flowing from different climates, different soils,
different productions, different modes of existence, and
its own local relations and duties, is made subservient to
all the petty interests of the other, to *their* laws, *their*
regulations, *their* passions and wars, and interdicted from
social intercourse, from the interchange of mutual duties and comforts with their neighbors, enjoined on all
men by the laws of nature.   Happily these abuses of

human rights are drawing to a close on both our continents, and are not likely to survive the present mad contest of the lions and tigers of the other.

* * *

We cannot too distinctly detach ourselves from the European system, which is essentially belligerent, nor too sedulously cultivate an American system, essentially pacific. But if we go into commercial treaties at all, they should be with all, at the same time, with whom we have important commercial relations.

* * *

Nothing is so important as that America shall separate herself from the systems of Europe and establish one of her own. Our circumstances, our pursuits, our interests, are distinct, the principles of our policy should be so also. All entanglements with that quarter of the globe should be avoided if we mean that peace and justice shall be the polar stars of the American societies.

* * *

I have ever deemed it fundamental for the United States, never to take active part in the quarrels of Europe. Their political interests are entirely distinct from ours. Their mutual jealousies, their balance of power, their complicated alliances, their forms and principles of government, are all foreign to us. They are nations of eternal war. All their energies are expended in the destruction of the labor, property and lives of their people. On our part, never had a people so favorable a chance of trying the opposite system, of peace and fraternity with mankind, and the direction of all our means and faculties to the purposes of improvement instead of destruction. With Europe we have few occasions of collision, and these, with a little prudence and forbearance, may be generally accommodated. Of the brethren of our own hemisphere, none are yet, or for an age to come will be, in a shape, condition, or disposition to war against us. And the foothold which the nations of Europe had in either America, is slipping from under them, so that we shall soon be rid of their neighborhood. Cuba alone seems at present to hold up a speck of war to us. Its possession by Great Britain would indeed be a great calamity to us. Could we induce her to join us in guaranteeing its independence against all the world, *except* Spain, it would be nearly as valuable to us as if it were our own.

* * *

Our first and fundamental maxim should be, never to entangle ourselves in the broils of Europe. Our second, never to suffer Europe to intermeddle with cis-Atlantic affairs. America, North and South, has a set of interests distinct from those of Europe, and peculiarly her own. She should therefore have a system of her own, separate and apart from that of Europe. While the last is laboring to become the domicil of despotism, our endeavor should surely be, to make our hemisphere that of freedom. One nation, most of all, could disturb us in this pursuit; she now offers to lead, aid, and accompany us in it. By acceding to her proposition, we detach her from the bands, bring her mighty weight into the scale of free government, and emancipate a continent at one stroke, which might otherwise linger long in doubt and difficulty. Great Britain is the nation which can do us the most harm of any one, or all on earth; and with her on our side we need not fear the whole world. With her then, we should most sedulously cherish a cordial friendship; and nothing would tend more to knit our affections than to be fighting once more, side by side, in the same cause. Not that I would purchase even her amity at the price of taking part in her wars. But the war in which the present proposition might engage us, should that be its consequence, is not her war, but ours. Its object is to introduce and establish the American system, of keeping out of our land all foreign powers, of never permitting those of Europe to intermeddle with the affairs of our nations. It is to maintain our own principle, not to depart from it. And if, to facilitate this, we can effect a division in the body of the European powers, and draw over to our side its most powerful member, surely we should do it.

* * *

Let us consecrate a sanctuary for those whom the misrule of Europe may compel to seek happiness in other climes. This refuge once known will produce reaction on the happiness even of those who remain there, by warning their task-masters that when the evils of Egyptian oppression become heavier than those of the abandonment of country, another Canaan is open where their subjects will be received as brothers, and secured against like oppressions by a participation in the right of self-government. If additional motives could be wanting with us to the maintenance of this right, they would be found in the animating consideration that a single good government becomes thus a blessing to the whole earth, its welcome to the oppressed restraining within certain limits the measure of their oppressions.

* * *

In the course of this conflict, let it be our endeavor, as it is our interest and desire, to cultivate the friendship of the belligerent nations by every act of justice and of incessant kindness ; to receive their armed vessels with hospitality from the distresses of the sea, but to administer the means of annoyance to none ; to establish in our harbors such a police as may maintain law and order ; to restrain our citizens from embarking individually in a war in which their country takes no part ; to punish severely those persons, citizen or alien, who shall usurp the cover of our flag for vessels not entitled to it, infecting thereby with suspicion those of real Americans, and committing us into controversies for the redress of wrongs not our own ; to exact from every nation the observance, toward our vessels and citizens, of those principles and practices which all civilized people acknowledge ; to merit the character of a just nation, and maintain that of an independent one, preferring every consequence to insult and habitual wrong.

Separated by a wide ocean from the nations of Europe, and from the political interests which entangle them together, with productions and wants which render our commerce and friendship useful to them and theirs to us, it cannot be the interest of any to assail us, nor ours to disturb them. We should be most unwise, indeed, were we to cast away the singular blessings of the position in which nature has placed us, the opportunity she has endowed us with of pursuing, at a distance from foreign contentions, the paths of industry, peace, and happiness ; of cultivating general friendship, and of bringing collisions of interest to the umpirage of reason rather than of force.

* * *

We certainly cannot deny to other nations that principle whereon our government is founded, that every nation has a right to govern itself internally under what forms it pleases, and to change these forms at its own will ; and externally to transact business with other nations through whatever organ it chooses, whether that be a King, Convention, Assembly, Committee, President, or whatever it be. The only thing essential is, the

will of the nation.   Taking this as your polar star, you *
can hardly err.

* * *

I am sensible that your † situation must have been difficult during the transition from the late form of government to the re-establishment of some other legitimate authority, and that you may have been at a loss to
determine with whom business might be done.   Nevertheless, when principles are well understood, their application is less embarrassing.   We surely cannot deny
to any nation that right whereon our own government
is founded, that every one may govern itself according
to whatever form it pleases, and change these forms at
its own will ; and that it may transact its business with
foreign nations through whatever organ it thinks proper,
whether King, Convention, Assembly, Committee, President, or anything else it may choose.   The will of the
nation is the only thing essential to be regarded.

* * *

In the whole animal kingdom I recollect no family
but man, steadily and systematically employed in the
destruction of itself.   Nor does what is called civilization produce any other effect, than to teach him to pursue the principle of the *bellum omnium in omnia* on a
greater scale, and instead of the little contest between
tribe and tribe, to comprehend all the quarters of the
earth in the same work of destruction.   If to this we
add, that as to other animals, the lions and tigers are
mere lambs compared with man as a destroyer, we must
conclude that nature has been able to find in man alone
a sufficient barrier against the too great multiplication
of other animals and of man himself, an equilibrating
power against the fecundity of generation.

* * *

* Thomas Pinckney.   † Gouverneur Morris.

If we are forced into war, we must give up political differences of opinion, and unite as one man to defend our country. But whether at the close of such a war, we should be as free as we are now, God knows. In fine, if war takes place, republicanism has everything to fear ; if peace, be assured that your forebodings and my alarms will prove vain ; and that the spirit of our citizens now rising as rapidly as it was then running crazy, and rising with a strength and majesty which show the loveliness of freedom, will make this government in practice, what it is in principle, a model for the protection of man in a state of *freedom* and *order*.

* * *

The two last Congresses have been the theme of the most licentious reprobation for printers thirsting after war, some against France and some against England. But the people wish for peace with both. They feel no incumbency on them to become the reformers of the other hemisphere, and to inculcate, with fire and sword, a return to moral order. When, indeed, peace shall become more losing than war, they may owe to their interests what these Quixotes are clamoring for on false estimates of honor.

* * *

Another great field of political experiment is opening in our neighborhood, in Spanish America. I fear the degrading ignorance into which their priests and kings have sunk them, has disqualified them from the maintenance or even knowledge of their rights, and that much blood may be shed for little improvement in their condition. Should their new rulers honestly lay their shoulders to remove the great obstacles of ignorance, and press the remedies of education and information, they will still be in jeopardy until another generation comes into place, and what may happen in the interval cannot be predicted, nor shall you * or I live to see it.

* * *

Spanish America is all in revolt. The insurgents are triumphant in many of the States, and will be so in all. But there the danger is that the cruel arts of their oppressors have enchained their minds, have kept them in the ignorance of children, and as incapable of self-government as children. If the obstacles of bigotry and priest-craft can be surmounted, we may hope that common-sense will suffice to do everything else. God send them a safe deliverance.

* * *

HISTORY AND THE CONTEMPORARY WORLD

I agree with you in all its † eulogies on the eighteenth century. It certainly witnessed the sciences and arts, manners and morals, advanced to a higher degree than the world had ever before seen. And might we not go back to the æra of the Borgias, by which time the barbarous ages had reduced national morality to its lowest point of depravity, and observe that the arts and sciences, rising from that point, advanced gradually through all the sixteenth, seventeenth and eighteenth centuries, softening and correcting the manners and morals of man ? I think, too, we may add to the great honor of science and the arts, that their natural effect is, by illuminating public opinion, to erect it into a censor, before which the most exalted tremble for their future, as well as present fame. With some exceptions only, through the seventeenth and eighteenth centuries,

* M. Dupont de Nemours.
† John Adams' letter of November 13, 1815.

morality occupied an honorable chapter in the political code of nations. You must have observed while in Europe, as I thought I did, that those who administered the governments of the greater powers at least, had a respect to faith, and considered the dignity of their government as involved in its integrity.

How then has it happened that these nations, France especially and England, so great, so dignified, so distinguished by science and the arts, plunged all at once into all the depths of human enormity, threw off suddenly and openly all the restraints of morality, all sensation to character, and unblushingly avowed and acted on the principle that power was right? Can this sudden apostasy from national rectitude be accounted for? The treaty of Pilnitz seems to have begun it, suggested perhaps by the baneful precedent of Poland. Was it from the terror of monarchs, alarmed at the light returning on them from the west, and kindling a volcano under their thrones? Was it a combination to extinguish that light, and to bring back, as their best auxiliaries, those enumerated by you, the Sorbonne, the Inquisition, the Index Expurgatorius, and the knights of Loyola? Whatever it was, the close of the century saw the moral world thrown back again to the age of the Borgias, to the point from which it had departed three hundred years before. But although your prophecy has proved true so far, I hope it does not preclude a better final result. That same light from our west seems to have spread and illuminated the very engines employed to extinguish it. It has given them a glimmering of their rights and their power. The idea of representative government has taken root and growth among them. Their masters feel it, and are saving themselves by timely offers of this modification of their powers. Belgium, Prussia, Poland, Lombardy, &c., are now offered a representative organization; illusive probably at first, but it will grow into power in the end. Opinion is power, and that opinion will come.

There are three epochs in history, signalized by the total extinction of national morality. The first was of the successors of Alexander, not omitting himself : The next, the successors of the first Cæsar : The third, our own age. This was begun by the partition of Poland, followed by that of the treaty of Pilnitz ; next the conflagration of Copenhagen ; then the enormities of Bonaparte, partitioning the earth at his will, and devastating it with fire and sword ; now the conspiracy of Kings, the successors of Bonaparte, blasphemously calling themselves the Holy Alliance, and treading in the footsteps of their incarcerated leader ; not yet, indeed, usurping the government of other nations, avowedly and in detail, but controlling by their armies the forms in which they will permit them to be governed.

* * *

Here I discontinue my relation of the French Revolution. The minuteness with which I have so far given its details, is disproportioned to the general scale of my narrative. But I have thought it justified by the interest which the whole world must take in this Revolution. As yet, we are but in the first chapter of its history. The appeal to the rights of man, which had been made in the United States, was taken up by France, first of the European nations. From her, the spirit has spread over those of the South. The tyrants of the North have allied indeed against it ; but it is irresistible. Their opposition will only multiply its millions of human victims ; their own satellites will catch it, and the condition of man through the civilized world, will be finally and greatly ameliorated. This is a wonderful instance of great events from small causes. So inscrutable is the arrangement of causes and consequences in this world, that a two-penny duty on tea, unjustly imposed in a sequestered part of it, changes the condition of all its inhabitants.

* * *

Happy for us that abuses have not yet become patrimonies, and that every description of interest is in favor of national and moderate government. That we are yet able to send our wise and good men together to talk over our form of government, discuss its weaknesses and establish its remedies with the same *sang-froid* as they would a subject of agriculture. The example we have given to the world is single, that of changing our form of government under the authority of reason only, without bloodshed.

* * *

You * say you are not sufficiently informed about the nature and circumstances of the present struggle here.† Having been on the spot from its first origin, and watched its movements as an uninterested spectator, with no other bias than a love of mankind, I will give you my ideas of it. Though celebrated writers of this and other countries had already sketched good principles on the subject of government, yet the American war seems first to have awakened the thinking part of this nation in general from the sleep of despotism in which they were sunk. The officers too who had been to America, were mostly young men, less shackled by habit and prejudice, and more ready to assent to the dictates of common sense and common right. They came back impressed with these. The press, notwithstanding its shackles, began to disseminate them ; conversation, too, assumed new freedom ; politics became the theme of all societies, male and female, and a very extensive and zealous party was formed, which may be called the

* Dr. Richard Price.
† Paris.

Patriotic party, who, sensible of the abusive government under which they lived, longed for occasions of reforming it. This party comprehended all the honesty of the kingdom, sufficiently at its leisure to think ; the men of letters, the easy bourgeois, the young nobility, partly from reflection, partly from mode ; for those sentiments became a matter of mode, and as such united most of the young women to the party.

* * *

So far it seemed that your revolution had got along with a steady peace ; meeting indeed occasional difficulties and dangers, but we are not to expect to be translated from despotism to liberty in a feather-bed. I have never feared for the ultimate result, though I have feared for you * personally.

* * *

In the struggle which was necessary, many guilty persons fell without the forms of trial, and with them some innocent. These I deplore as much as any body, and shall deplore some of them to the day of my death. But I deplore them as I should have done had they fallen in battle. It was necessary to use the arm of the people, a machine not quite so blind as balls and bombs, but blind to a certain degree. A few of their cordial friends met at their hands the fate of enemies. But time and truth will rescue and embalm their memories, while their posterity will be enjoying that very liberty for which they would never have hesitated to offer up their lives. The liberty of the whole earth was depending on the issue of the contest, and was ever such a prize won with so little innocent blood ? My own affections have been deeply wounded by some of the martyrs to this cause, but rather than it should have failed I would have

* Marquis de Lafayette.

seen half the earth desolated ; were there but an Adam and an Eve left in every country, and left free, it would be better than as it now is.

* * *

You * have understood that the revolutionary movements in Europe had, by industry and artifice, been wrought into objects of terror even to this country, and had really involved a great portion of our well-meaning citizens in a panic which was perfectly unaccountable, and during the prevalence of which they were led to support measures the most insane. They are now pretty thoroughly recovered from it, and sensible of the mischief which was done, and preparing to be done, had their minds continued a little longer under that derangement.

* * *

Much to their credit, however, unshackled by the prejudices which chain down the minds of the common mass of Europe, the experiment has proved that, where thought is free in its range, we need never fear to hazard what is good in itself. This sample of the American mind is an additional item for the flattering picture your letter presents of our situation, and our prospects. I firmly believe in them all ; and that human nature has never looked forward, under circumstances so auspicious, either for the sum of happiness, or the spread of surface provided to receive it. Very contrary opinions are inculcated in Europe, and in England especially, where I much doubt if you would be tolerated in presenting the views you propose. The English have been a wise, a virtuous and truly estimable people. But commerce and a corrupt government have rotted them to the core. Every generous, nay, every just sentiment, is

* Joel Barlow.

absorbed in the thirst for gold. I speak of their cities, which we may certainly pronounce to be ripe for despotism, and fitted for no other government.

* * *

Who could have imagined that the two most distinguished in the rank of nations, for science and civilization, would have suddenly descended from that honorable eminence, and setting at defiance all those moral laws established by the Author of nature between nation and nation, as between man and man, would cover earth and sea with robberies and piracies, merely because strong enough to do it with temporal impunity ; and that under this disbandment of nations from social order, we should have been despoiled of a thousand ships, and have thousands of our citizens reduced to Algerine slavery. Yet all this has taken place.

* * *

When I left France at the close of '89, your * revolution was, as I thought, under the direction of able and honest men. But the madness of some of their successors, the vices of others, the malicious intrigues of an envious and corrupting neighbor, the tracasserie of the Directory, the usurpations, the havoc, and devastations of your Attila, and the equal usurpations, depredations and oppressions of your hypocritical deliverers, will form a mournful period in the history of man, a period of which the last chapter will not be seen in your day or mine, and one which I still fear is to be written in characters of blood. Had Bonaparte reflected that such is the moral construction of the world, that no national crime passes unpunished in the long run, he would not now be in the cage of St. Helena ; and were your present oppressors to reflect on the same truth, they would spare to their own countries the penalties on their present wrongs which will be inflicted on them on future times.

* French. Written to Baron Humboldt.

The seeds of hatred and revenge which they are now sowing with a large hand, will not fail to produce their fruits in time. Like their brother robbers on the highway, they suppose the escape of the moment a final escape, and deem infamy and future risk countervailed by present gain.

* * *

The generation which commences a revolution rarely completes it. Habituated from their infancy to passive submission of body and mind to their kings and priests, they are not qualified when called on to think and provide for themselves ; and their inexperience, their ignorance and bigotry make them instruments often, in the hands of the Bonapartes and Iturbides, to defeat their own rights and purposes. This is the present situation of Europe and Spanish America. But it is not desperate. The light which has been shed on mankind by the art of printing, has eminently changed the condition of the world. As yet, that light has dawned on the middling classes only of the men in Europe. The kings and the rabble, of equal ignorance, have not yet received its rays ; but it continues to spread, and while printing is preserved, it can no more recede than the sun return on his course. A first attempt to recover the right of self-government may fail, so may a second, a third, &c. But as a younger and more instructed race comes on, the sentiment becomes more and more intuitive, and a fourth, a fifth, or some subsequent one of the ever renewed attempts will ultimately succeed. In France, the first effort was defeated by Robespierre, the second by Bonaparte, the third by Louis XVIII. and his holy allies : another is yet to come, and all Europe, Russia excepted, has caught the spirit ; and all will attain representative government, more or less perfect. This is now well understood to be a necessary check on kings, whom they will probably think it more prudent to chain and tame, than to exterminate. To attain all this, however, rivers of blood must yet flow, and years of desolation pass over ; yet the object is worth rivers of blood, and years of desolation. For what inheritance so valuable, can man leave to his posterity ? You * and I shall look down from another world on these glorious achievements of man, which will add to the joys even of heaven.

* * *

I am eighty-one years of age, born where I now live, in the first range of mountains in the interior of our country. And I have observed this march of civilization advancing from the sea coast, passing over us like a cloud of light, increasing our knowledge and improving our condition, insomuch as that we are at this time more advanced in civilization here than the seaports were when I was a boy. And where this progress will stop no one can say. Barbarism has, in the meantime, been receding before the steady step of amelioration ; and will in time, I trust, disappear from the earth. You † seem to think that this advance has brought on too complicated a state of society, and that we should gain in happiness by treading back our steps a little way. I think, myself, that we have more machinery of government than is necessary, too many parasites living on the labor of the industrious. I believe it might be much simplified to the relief of those who maintain it.

* * *

May it ‡ be to the world, what I believe it will be, (to some part sooner, to others later, but finally to all,) the signal of arousing men to burst the chains under which monkish ignorance and superstition had persuaded them to bind themselves, and to assume the blessings and se-

* John Adams.
† Wm. Ludlow.
‡ The Declaration of Independence.

curity of self-government. That form which we have substituted, restores the free right to the unbounded exercise of reason and freedom of opinion. All eyes are opened, or opening, to the rights of man. The general spread of the light of science has already laid open to every view the palpable truth, that the mass of mankind has not been born with saddles on their backs, nor a favored few booted and spurred, ready to ride them legitimately, by the grace of God. These are grounds of hope for others.